Working with Stress and Tension in Clinical Practice

Working with Stress and Tension in Clinical Practice is a practical toolkit that sets out a wide range of approaches for reducing stress and anxiety in clients so that they are mentally prepared for more effective therapy sessions. Combining research, real-life examples and practical advice, the book discusses the potential psychological barriers to therapy that can stand in the way of helping clients and offers concrete solutions to overcome these issues. This toolkit clearly outlines a range of approaches such as mindfulness and meditation techniques that can help clients focus on their therapy and overcome stress and anxiety.

Key features include:

- Guidance and activities supporting the use of meditation, breathing exercises and visualisation techniques in therapy

- Ideas that can be used as short introductory activities at the beginning of a therapy session to help patients get the most from the therapist's time

- Suggested whole sessions on stress reduction for those focusing on anxiety itself.

This book is a must-have resource for Speech and Language Therapists, Occupational Therapists, Psychologists, Counsellors, Psychotherapists and any professionals working with clients who wish to help the people they work with get the most from therapy.

Helen Morris has worked as a Speech and Language Therapist for many years in hospitals, clinics and community settings, in the UK and internationally. She has extensive experience of the need to help patients overcome anxiety and other emotional obstacles that stand in the way of effective therapy.

Working with Stress and Tension in Clinical Practice

A Practical Guide for Therapists

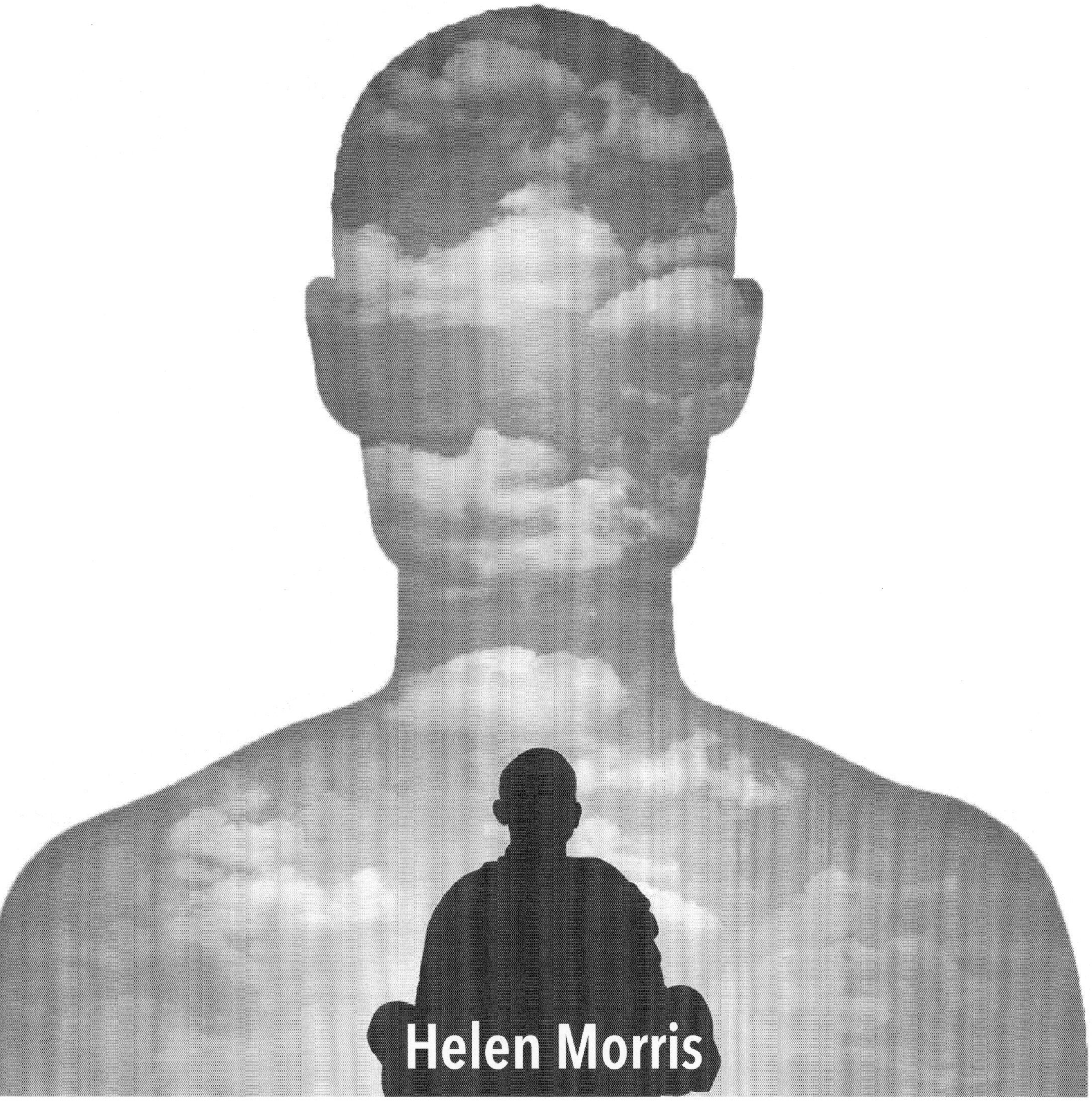

Helen Morris

LONDON AND NEW YORK

First published 2018
by Routledge
2 Park Square, Milton Park, Abingdon, Oxon OX14 4RN

and by Routledge
711 Third Avenue, New York, NY 10017

Routledge is an imprint of the Taylor & Francis Group, an informa business

British Library Cataloguing-in-Publication Data
A catalogue record for this book is available from the British Library

Library of Congress Cataloging-in-Publication Data
Names: Morris, Helen, 1981– author.
Title: Working with stress and tension in clinical practice : a practical guide for therapists / Helen Morris.
Description: Abingdon, Oxon ; New York, NY : Routledge, 2018. | Includes bibliographical references.
Identifiers: LCCN 2017029020 (print) | LCCN 2017031886 (ebook) | ISBN 9781315172491 (ebook) | ISBN 9781911186274 (pbk.) | ISBN 9781315172491 (ebk.)
Subjects: | MESH: Stress, Psychological—therapy | Clinical Medicine | Patients—psychology | Patient Acceptance of Health Care | Psychotherapeutic Processes | Professional-Patient Relations
Classification: LCC RC467 (ebook) | LCC RC467 (print) | NLM WM 172.4 | DDC 616.89—dc23
LC record available at https://lccn.loc.gov/2017029020

ISBN: 978-1-911186-27-4 (pbk)
ISBN: 978-1-315-17249-1 (ebk)

Typeset in VAG Rounded
by Apex CoVantage, LLC

I would like to thank my partner Paul and son Rohan for giving me the time and space to write this book; there is no way I could have written it without their support.

I would also like to gratefully acknowledge my brother Leo and friend since childhood, Christine Wilkinson, who between them have helped point me in the direction of meditation, mindfulness and conscious parenting through recommending books and providing opportunities to discuss and explore ideas further.

I am indebted to Gail Fahey, Emma Cooper, Lizi McGarvey and Rachael Atkinson for reviewing the proposal and particularly to Gail and Emma who read the manuscript and gave wonderful support and feedback – I really appreciated all your help and encouragement!

To Gail, I miss our discussions on mindfulness and consciousness, but sincerely hope you are enjoying living consciously in Spain!

Contents

Acknowledgements

I would like to express my genuine appreciation to Emilie Coin, my Editorial Assistant at Speechmark, for helping me through this process, particularly with regards to gaining permissions, and also to Ben Hulme-Cross at Speechmark for giving me the opportunity to write this book.

I would like to sincerely thank Patrick McKeown, Patricia Worby and Kit Malia for reading and reviewing chapters and giving me invaluable feedback – I am extremely grateful to you all for taking the time to do this.

I want to acknowledge how much all the amazing books I have referenced have helped guide me with this book. I feel fortunate to have found them; they have been inspirational and I recommend reading them all.

Many, many thanks also to the following for permission to use quotations from the following texts in the book:

Vision for Life: Ten Steps to Natural Eyesight Improvement, by Meir Schneider, published by North Atlantic Books, copyright © 2012 by Meir Schneider. Reprinted by permission of North Atlantic Books.

You Can Be Happy, Daniel Freeman and Jason Freeman, Pearson Education Limited © Daniel Freeman and Jason Freeman 2012. Reprinted with permission of publisher.

The Healing Power of the Human Voice, by James D'Angelo, PhD, published by Inner Traditions International and Bear & Company, © 2005. All rights reserved.

www.Innertraditions.com Reprinted with permission of publisher.

- Patrick McKeown (Patrick McKeown.net)
- Patricia Worby
- Louise L. Hay (Hay House)
- Anita Moorjani (Hay House)
- Michael Neill (Hay House)
- Bruce H. Lipton PhD (Hay House)
- David R. Hamilton PhD (Hay House)

- Dr Joe Dispenza (Hay House)
- Bronnie Ware (Hay House)
- Annemarie Postma (Watkins Publishing)
- Mike George (Duncan Baird Publishers)
- Dr Antonio Jimenez (The Truth about Cancer)
- Dennis Greenberger and Christine A. Padesky (Guildford Press)
- Dr Chris Williams (CRC Press)

Introduction

During the course of my practice as a Speech Therapist, I have observed that with the majority of clients getting down to the business of therapy is not straightforward. It is usually impeded and obstructed by clients' divided attention; this is not, however, just because of cognitive impairment. Clients come to us because they need help; they are at a difficult time in their lives, and because of this they not only have their impairments to deal with, but also their emotional reactions to cope with too. In our society we have not been taught how to cope with our thinking mind – our runaway thoughts – or to confront our emotions and process them in a constructive way. Consequently when clients reach this challenging time, they are not always well equipped to deal with it.

This can result in spiralling stress and tension. Consequently clients can become stuck in their minds – locked in a cycle of worrying thoughts, making attending to therapy very difficult to near impossible.

This book aims to address this key issue of working through a client's processing of their situation and bring their attention back to therapy in order to achieve optimal therapy outcomes. It is intended for therapists to help clients reduce stress and fear – which is felt as tension throughout the body and mind. The worries and tensions can take hold of clients and hijack their attention. This can significantly affect their ability to perform optimally in assessments and therapy and achieve the best possible outcomes. Therefore therapists are not able to get an accurate assessment of the client – clients are unknowingly disabling themselves. It also severely impacts on their quality of life.

I hope to highlight the importance of working on tension and stress, and encourage therapists to allow the time to do this within therapy sessions. This resource will aim to give therapists the confidence to reach out and connect with clients on a deeper level. To metaphorically take clients by the hand and explore their feelings and to enable them to find the space, the stillness and the peace that IS within them, and is ALWAYS there. However, this stillness is usually concealed, not only in our clients but in everyone, by the layers that we add – the tensions, the stresses, the distractions – the thinking mind. By rediscovering this peace, this sanctuary, clients create a space inside themselves in order to process information much more effectively. It is my intention that they will also rediscover joy. This I hope will give them new energy to move forward in a positive way and accept and embrace life.

This book covers a variety of related topics which can all increase a patient's self-awareness and confidence to take control of their emotions and their psychological well-being. It will allow clients to gain a new perspective into themselves and take away the fear of the unknown/the darkness within themselves. Clients can be empowered by being taught ways to reduce their tension. The methods are simple and effective, and most clients become increasingly interested even when initially very reticent.

These are not new ideas but merely presented in a new way specifically with the aim of being put to use with clients. I hope it helps therapists understand their clients better, and increases their awareness of the benefits of helping clients relax and reduce their stress. By compassionately working through this surmountable barrier together (the clients' thinking and emotions), therapists can guide clients to reach their potential.

I sincerely hope this resource stimulates an interest in therapists to learn more about mindfulness and understanding themselves and their own thoughts and emotions. To do this is to trigger a change in consciousness, so that it is more automatic in their interactions with clients and everyone around them. To live consciously is to live more productively, creatively and peacefully both within ourselves and among others. If client and therapist can do this, the therapeutic process would be maximised and rewarding for both parties. I hope therefore that this resource will also benefit therapists personally. If therapists see the benefits in their own lives it will inspire them further to use it more widely with their clients.

1. Identifying barriers to therapy

Understanding each client and their internal obstructions (fears and uncertainties) to therapy allows therapists to work more effectively with them.

Aims

- To understand potential psychological barriers to therapy.

- To understand how to identify barriers.

A client's readiness to engage

"Getting going" with therapy can be challenging in many cases. Clients can be difficult to engage with in the therapy process. This may happen initially, throughout the course of intervention or occur sporadically. Clients may be completely resistant to any intervention from the outset, they may not put their full effort into therapy, they may respond with "No. I can't." when new suggestions or activities are introduced, there may be poor compliance with completing the tasks you provide between sessions and there may be hesitancy in attempting carry-over of new skills to real-life situations outside the therapy session (even if you are confident they can manage this).

We meet clients because they need support, so why are they holding back from the support you are trying to give?

Reactions

When we see clients they are at a vulnerable point in their lives. We are seeing them for a particular, possibly new issue. However, the "problem" is more than just the impairment or disease. The "problem" is immediately and inextricably connected to the client's reaction to it. The reaction is usually a problem in itself and often eclipses the original issue; clients thereby more than double their problem.

A client's reactions (thoughts, feelings and beliefs) about their situation are the first aspect to be focused on, as this is where the resistance to therapy lies. Reactions are instant and can be difficult to move on from, clients can get "stuck" in their panic and despair and this is what shapes their responses or lack thereof. If a client's thoughts are dominated by the stresses and tensions that consume them, they become psychological barriers. A true understanding of a client's abilities and potential cannot be gained. We need to differentiate between the initial "problem" and the reactions which cause additional limitations. How much more could a client achieve and how much further could they progress without those limitations? How much are they limiting themselves? Any impairment or "problem" which they come to you with then is not the initial problem to work on but the psychological barrier.

Reactions come from our past

Reactions are heavily influenced by our past experiences, our background, our childhood, and our culture and religion which guide our thinking and form our beliefs (see also chapter: "An Introduction to Mindfulness for Reducing Stress"). These factors are what we are all composed of and what have fundamentally shaped us unless we become conscious of them, consider them carefully and challenge them. These beliefs will also determine a client's openness to strangers and expectation about appointments, the process of therapy and outcomes. Additionally, clients will have unique character traits, abilities to learn and styles of learning, and they will also have their usual day-to-day concerns such as finances which add to their psychological load. Consequently, to maximise the opportunity you have for supporting a client with their difficulty, the client must be considered holistically to be understood better so that as a clinician you can support them more effectively. To do this they need to be observed with care, empathy and detachment. If they are not, all these other facets can potentially also become barriers to therapy.

Lack of awareness

Clients themselves may not understand they are creating barriers and inadvertently adding to their issues. Being immersed in and at the heart of the situation they are unlikely to have this perspective and insight; they would also be unaware they are able to change and control their reactions by developing their ability to respond. Reactions are unconscious responses.

We can all become more conscious of ourselves and our circumstances and take control of how we mentally respond, and we can teach clients to do this. The first step is to be aware of the resistance coming from within the client and encourage them to develop this awareness of themselves in order to then let go and move on in therapy. It may be the case, however, that on understanding these barriers you realise that your intervention is not appropriate at this time.

Examples of psychological barriers to therapy

- Low motivation.

- Impairment/issue not severe enough for patient to warrant the effort required in therapy.

- Emotions – low mood/depression/self-pity, fear, anxiety, anger, guilt, shame, embarrassment, frustration.

- Reduced confidence.

- Harsh self-criticism.

- Non-acceptance of situation.

- Resignation/giving up.

- Unused to/unwilling to take responsibility for themselves – expectations of health care professionals providing a "quick fix".

- Lack of trust in therapist.

- Character trait – prefers to talk/do it their way rather than listen to information and follow advice.

- Other issues pre-dominate consciousness.

- Not feeling understood by therapist – misunderstandings of therapist.

- Age/cultural differences of client/therapist.

- Lack of family support.

Case examples of reactions and barriers to therapy

OS

OS was an elderly widow living alone. She was registered blind. However, she continued to run a small guest house in her home, mainly taking in foreign students. She had two daughters who did not live nearby.

OS had just been discharged home from hospital following a stroke. OS also immediately resumed the running of her guest house which involved not only making breakfasts but also dinners. When guests were out for the day she would always find things to do, tiring herself out. Her fatigue was impacting therapy sessions.

Identifying barriers to therapy

When this was discussed, OS reported feeling that she couldn't allow herself to sit down and rest, "doing nothing" made her feel guilty and agitated. OS only felt ok about herself if engaged in activity. There was no flexibility in her thinking. Her beliefs lead to high expectations and demands of herself without taking into account her recent stroke. She had not questioned if that was reasonable.

CS

CS was a retired woman who had had a stroke. She welcomed support and was usually very motivated. Low mood was an issue for CS at times but she could be jovial and was generally open to therapy. From time to time, however, there was complete resistance to therapy, like a brick wall had suddenly gone up. This was in response to feeling like she was being pushed into doing therapy tasks she did not like to do as she did not enjoy them, did not feel she could do them and did not want to expose these weaknesses, and she also did not believe they would help her.

The barriers were her mood, fears and misunderstandings. This resulted in her retreating into herself away from the therapist – her attention was away from the therapy and focused on her negative feelings, and it was very hard to pull her attention away from them.

JC

JC was a palliative client. He had significant swallowing difficulties (dysphagia). JC needed a modified diet to reduce the risk of aspiration pneumonia; he was also recommended exercises to strengthen the muscles involved in swallowing. JC lived with his wife who had advanced dementia. He welcomed therapists into his home; his pleasures came from talking to visitors, watching programmes about World War II and eating the food he liked.

JC was not compliant with either the dietary advice or the exercises. This lack of compliance was due to complete acceptance. JC understood his situation; he was aware of what he was doing and he was making choices. His priority was short-term pleasures.

BM

BM was retired. He was visited at home for six weeks following his stroke. BM was resistant to therapy throughout most of the course of intervention. He was able to engage to a degree, but often became irritable: he wasn't able to concentrate on tasks and explore his full potential as a result.

BM behaved like this in therapy because he was guarded. BM was embarrassed about his weaknesses and also fearful of exploring the depth and range of them with a stranger.

LS

LS was a young woman who had mild impairments following a stroke. She was unable to fully engage in therapy as she had more significant housing and relationship issues to think of. These matters subsequently dominated sessions. The impairment was not significant enough to concern her compared to these other worries.

KS

KS was highly anxious following his stroke. He was retired and lived with his wife who was also just as anxious about their changed circumstances.

KS was grief stricken. His impairments were significant, and the stroke was very recent. He was overwhelmed by his emotions but he also had to deal with his wife's, which dominated the therapy sessions due to her ability to articulate them more easily. KS was unable to accept what had happened to him and he was locked in his all-encompassing despair. It took six weeks to work on this in order to prepare him for beginning to work on the impairments.

DB

DB was elderly and lived alone. She had relatively mild impairments following her recent stroke. She was evidently highly anxious when attempting therapy exercises. DB was terrified about getting things wrong, and her anxiety hijacked her ability to focus on tasks. It was this anxiety that was the primary barrier.

Contrast with these case examples

BH

BH was young and in employment prior to his stroke. He lived alone but had supportive family nearby. BH had mild-moderate communication impairments.

From the outset BH engaged fully in therapy. He had insight into his difficulties and was very motivated to improve in order to return to work.

DI

DI was recently retired, but led an active life with her various hobbies and helping with the care of her grandchildren.

Following her stroke which left her with moderate communication impairments she was keen to improve and return to her everyday activities and resume her role within the family.

DB

DB had mild impairments following his recent stroke. He was a retired widower but had a large supportive family who all lived locally. He was also actively involved in his church and enjoyed going out on the train for days out independently. He was keen to return to resuming this life.

DB was open to seeing therapists, and fully focused on participating in all therapy tasks.

Common factors which contributed to openness to the therapy process

- An ability to accept situation enough to move focus on to dealing with their difficulties.

- An ability to manage anxieties sufficiently to explore impairments – degree and range of.

- Insight into problems and need to engage to maximise outcomes.

- Having reasons to be highly motivated to do as well as possible, e.g. return to work, leisure activities and resume role within family.

- Trust in the therapist.

- Well supported by family.

- Mood sufficiently positive to not be consumed by negative emotions.

How to identify potential psychological barriers to therapy

- Do you sense tension, stress, worries (facial expressions, body language, do they appear nervous, have you observed obsessive negative thinking)?

- Is the client distracted by them?

- Is the client avoiding doing therapy tasks?

- Is work set between sessions unfinished/not attempted?

- Is performance in therapy tasks variable?

- Does the patient behave in a hostile manner?

- Does the patient lack or appear to lack a sense of seriousness/gravity regarding their difficulty (patient not taking time to think when asked questions or doing activities, preferring to joke their way through, perhaps to mask their difficulties)?

Once you have identified the potential barriers you can start to support your client to deal with them; you will then be able to move forward effectively with the therapy process.

Summary

- Clients may not be ready to fully engage in therapy due to psychological barriers.

- We react to situations based on our programming – our conditioning in childhood.

- Understanding that clients may be holding back for a variety of reasons, which they may not be aware of and/or unwilling to discuss, can help you to approach the situation with care, patience and compassion.

2. Introducing the idea of working on negative thinking, stress and relaxation

Directing clients to attend to their feelings of stress and tension can help them to be with them and move through them.

Aims

- To understand how to explore the subject of working on stress and relaxation with clients.

- To increase confidence in working on stress and tension with clients.

- To understand how a few minutes taken to work on stress can have a significant effect on clients and therapy.

Raising the subject of stress is not something you want to go wading into straight away with a client, to give it a go and try to make clients feel better. Clients can ultimately only help themselves with this, as only they think in their minds; they have to be ready and open to consider this. Depending on your profession, experience and your remit in any particular therapeutic situation, you can take discussions to a deeper level or you can keep things simple by gently introducing general ideas for clients to reflect on or just providing opportunities for them to experience practising relaxation techniques, to connect with what they already have within – stillness.

What is encouraged in this book is ultimately about the client reducing stress and tension by observing and understanding themselves more, and finding the space they have inside. Spending time in this space allows your client to experience what they are already capable of – finding inner peace. With this experience comes increased inner strength – they don't need anything or anyone for this, they already have it, you are simply pointing this out. Through finding this stillness, they can clear their mind and thus free it for therapy. They will be more open and attentive when their mind is calm and not preoccupied with worries or even day-to-day matters. The primary and most profound way of doing this is through a guided meditation or visualisation, with minimal introduction if you sense a client is not open to disclosing anything about how they are feeling, as this peace and stillness is beyond words.

A simple guided meditation or visualisation such as *The Beach* visualisation (see chapter: "Visualisation") is in fact a very effective place to begin for stress reduction. Most clients, although unsure about it, will usually allow you take up 5–10 minutes at the end of a session to try it. You and your client may be surprised at their response at the end of the meditation. Often you may see a very different expression on their face – more calm, but also slightly curious, as they reflect on how the experience had more of an effect on them than they had anticipated. You may then find increasingly more time is spent doing guided meditations – they have discovered something inside themselves that they may not have been in contact with for a long time. Also, they may well be more open to talking more freely about their stress levels following this.

You can be the catalyst for encouraging a new way of being and thinking, and responding in therapy sessions. You can be the friendly guide, who is there to take them by the hand and help them look within themselves – something that many never do and may even find frightening to do, particularly by themselves. You can be there with your client, give them the permission and the courage to be in their mind and body fully. When you know that fears and worries are all just extra layers we have in our minds, and underneath is nothing – which is peace – it gives you the confidence to "go there", and take a peek inside yourself. When you are pleasantly surprised by the nothingness your fears about what is there inside of you need not concern you in the same way – you can go beyond them. "You" *are* what is beyond them.

You are unlikely to do anywhere near all that is suggested in this book with any one client. These are ideas and activities that you can internalise and introduce clients to and use as you feel is appropriate, based on your knowledge of the client, your experience, and what the situation calls for. If in doubt I would not attempt to work on stress reduction, but if you do decide to go ahead, just try a guided meditation. It may not be wise to push things with clients – some will be too resistant or just not ready at that time; for example they may be too absorbed by grief, their emotions may be too strong, or they are not able to attempt to sit and find the stillness. Then it is simply not appropriate. It all depends on the individual client.

The background information in this book may seem extensive and it may take several readings to understand some of the concepts. But the idea is to increase your understanding of your client and also yourself, and thereby your compassion for your client and your general approach to them which will help put them at ease. It will also help you to feel more confident about attempting stress reduction as part of your therapy. But you will always need to be aware of your limitations – know when to refer on to someone who is more skilled and experienced with the relevant issues, for example if a client is stuck in the grief cycle, then it would be more appropriate to refer them on to a trained counsellor or GP.

Summary

- As a therapist, you are in a position to introduce ways to reduce stress, and talk about clients' stresses where appropriate.

- Working on stress and tension can have a profound impact on clients.

- Taking a few minutes to work on reducing stress through a guided meditation may be all that is necessary to allow clients to benefit from working on relaxation, through which they can experience stillness.

3. Stress versus relaxation

From Meir Schneider, 2012, *Vision for Life: Ten Steps to Natural Eyesight Improvement*. Reprinted by permission of North Atlantic Books.

Aims

- To understand what stress is and how it is caused.

- To understand what relaxation is and the benefits of making time for it with clients.

- To learn ways of relaxing.

What is stress?

From Louise Hay, 2004, *I Can Do It*. Reprinted with permission.

Stress comes from our perception and management of events (whether everyday ones or larger life-changing ones). It is a "response to a situation or event in which you're put under pressure. It affects you emotionally and physically" (Hibberd and Usmar, 2014). These responses are generated by our fears – learnt fears (such as fear of social situations), and real ones (such as being chased by an aggressive dog) and even memories of or imaginary stressful situations – that is to say what we think is fearful, or what we perceive as threats. It also comes from having reduced confidence in ourselves – doubting that we are capable of meeting demands and expectations.

> We produce the stress, which is negative energy (because of our programming – how we have learnt to see the world); the situation does not itself generate it. The stress is in us, not our external reality.

The emotions and physical sensations are produced automatically in response to our thoughts and beliefs about the situation, which we don't feel in control of. The reactions can be experienced in our body – heart palpitations, sweating, hyperventilating, trembling, an inability to focus our eyes and of course muscle tension. Our thoughts are also already in overdrive but are then accelerated further in response to the uncomfortable feelings in our bodies. It's a vicious cycle. Our heads also feel tense and maybe we then start to experience a headache. But either way our minds are so gripped by what we are experiencing and seem so full that we have little or no room or capacity to think clearly. Therefore we can't make room for alternative thoughts which could improve the experience, to manipulate thoughts in order to get a different perspective, or to be confident that we can go on to manage it as effectively as possible.

To make things worse we immediately bring to mind similar experiences from the past – "the mind begins to trawl through memories to try and find something that will explain why we are feeling like this . . . and create[s] scenarios of what might happen in the future if we cannot explain what is going on now" (Williams and Penman, 2011). So not only do we have the now to deal with in our heads, but also the past *and* all sorts of worst-case scenarios about the future!

It is the old "fight or flight" response which is a protective mechanism, but paradoxically in the world we live in today it can often cause more harm than good. We end up feeling stuck, trapped and at the end of our tether even and not knowing how to begin to change things. How can we feel differently? How can we live differently?

What makes us perceive something as stressful?

As we experience the world differently (see chapter: "Understanding a Client's Experience of Reality"), what one person may experience as highly stressful may not affect another person at all, or only very slightly. Again it all comes down to our interpretation.

Stress and anxiety are also increasingly common problems in our society due to our faster-paced lifestyles and our ability and expectations to constantly stay in contact with the people in our lives, to "keep up" with everything that is happening, and to manage ever-demanding work-loads.

If only

We may think to ourselves such things as "if only I didn't have this to deal with", "if only I had more money", "if only I had a better job with more supportive colleagues". . . .

Life is not perfect for anyone. People with seemingly "better" lives – more money, a bigger house, better health, a "better" job, fame, and a "loving" family – all have their own stresses. Each individual's circumstance presents different issues (yes, even a "loving" family can inadvertently add pressures as we feel we want to do more for them/please them more, and we may want to be the person they want us to be to make them happy even though it is not really who we are – suppressing our true selves can cause stress). The stress symptoms are the same for anyone, the difference is how the situations are interpreted and the degree to which they are then felt.

Impact on progress in therapy

Your client will likely be experiencing a degree of stress. Stress causes tension throughout the body and mind; it uses up large amounts of energy (to maintain the tense muscles) and attention. It can be all-consuming, and overwhelming.

Attention, energy and positivity are key to successful therapy sessions. If a client is predominantly focused on their inner fears and anxieties and if the torment their body is going through is demanding more of their attention than what you are saying or doing, the client will not be functioning at their best and the outcomes of the session are less likely to be met.

The client is being disabled, and it is very hard to see how much at any given time. It will affect your confidence in your assessment and understanding of the client and their abilities. Perhaps you have lower expectations of them because you have only encountered them with their high levels of stress and you don't realise they could do more. The real client is masked behind the layers of tension and it can be very difficult to find them underneath.

Also, stress will impact on mood which will further impact on ability and enthusiasm. This helps to create a negative cycle of less-than-optimal performances in sessions, leading to more tension.

Stress conceals a client's potential because they are unable to concentrate effectively on anything outside themselves, when there is a storm going on within.

What is relaxation?

According to Lynn Marshall, "relaxation is a skill that we simply haven't been taught. . . . While we were growing up it wasn't regarded as important, necessary or desirable."

The feeling of relaxation is merely what is there when stress is not. It is the absence of something. It is not a thing we have to strive "to get"; it is already there when we haven't got the layers of fears and tensions that have accumulated. In fact, directly working on trying to be relaxed and attaching yourself to this inner state will only generate more stress. It is a by-product of things you are doing, such as mindfulness.

These layers build up significantly when we haven't kept on top of them, i.e. taken the time to relax so that we can come back down to our base-line level. If we can understand this and do this regularly (daily, and during and after stressful situations), we can keep on top of stress much better and enjoy a feeling of calm in our minds and throughout our whole bodies.

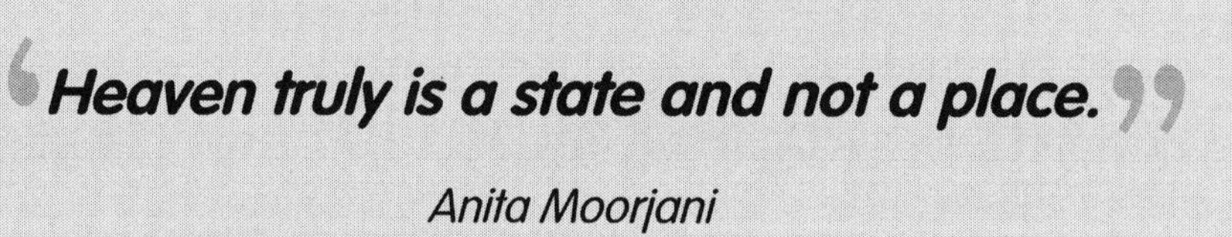

From Anita Moorjani, 2016, *What If This Is Heaven?* Reprinted with permission.

Benefits of relaxation and reducing stress

Relaxation is *necessary* to mentally and physically *prepare* ourselves for doing. What we do is more likely to be effective and carried out more efficiently when we are fully recharged and clear-headed so we can plan and make decisions.

Working on relaxation and stress reduction optimises clients' progress in therapy and improves quality of life. Clients will be free to engage without the distraction of their responses to stress. You will be able to get down to the business of therapy!

How to help clients manage their stress and relax?

> **❝It's not possible to have stress and inner harmony at the same time.❞**
>
> *Louise L. Hay*

From Louise Hay, 2004, *I Can Do It*. Reprinted with permission.

There is no one way to relax – there are many! Moreover, as Linda Blair (2014) writes, "Anyone can decide to release some tension and become more relaxed." It is actually more about doing things that allow you to relax rather than forcing it, which would in itself cause stress.

So the answer is to find ways of allowing relaxation; this will be individual to every person, just as one type of music can be painful for one person to listen to but can bring pleasure to someone else. Also remember clients may think they are relaxing at times but they are not; for example, when they are looking at their phones or watching TV. This is not true relaxation time given the compulsive nature of these activities, the fact that screens cause eye strain (leading to muscle tension) and also because what we see and hear can be causing stress in the body even if the client thinks they are enjoying it (just think of your responses when watching a thriller or any sports).

The key thing to remember is time – making time to really relax. Clients need to have regular opportunities to come down from stress and re-centre themselves. This can

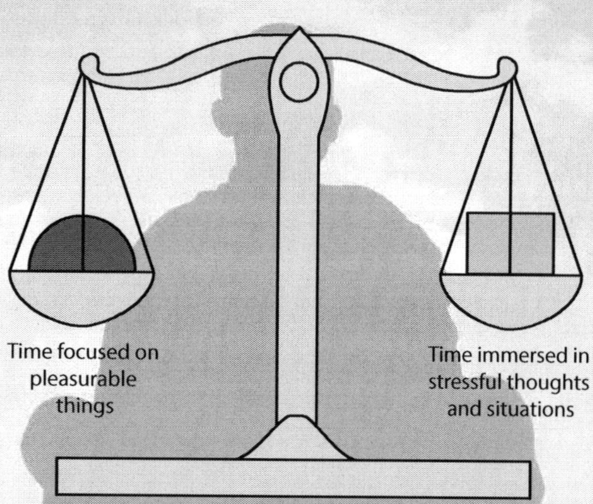

Figure 3.1 Balancing enjoyable things and fears

be done with the client using the relaxation activities below and throughout this book, but also as much as possible by appreciating pleasurable things (enjoying themselves) to counterbalance the stressful elements in life. If you are fully focused on enjoying yourself, you are not focused on the fear that is causing the stress and you are spending less time in a state of elevated tension. The balance needs to be in check or this state of tension becomes the norm, and you don't even realise it and completely forget what it feels like to be relaxed.

Summary

- Stress is caused by fears and feeling overwhelmed.

- It can be triggered by the situation we are in or a thought about a situation.

- Stress is very common in our society.

- Stress impacts on therapy – working on a client's stress will help them focus on therapy.

- Relaxation is the absence of stress; it can happen when we make time for activities we find relaxing.

- There are many ways to relax.

Activities

- Discuss what stress and relaxation is with client.

- Explore the client's stresses and the impact they may be having on therapy.

- Stretching – gentle head and neck.

- See activities in chapter: "An Introduction to Mindfulness for Reducing Stress".

- See activities in chapter: "The Breath".

- See activities in chapter: "Meditation".

- Explore what the client used to like to do – hobbies etc. long forgotten. Encourage them to remember what they liked doing as a child and what makes them laugh.

Guided meditations

- Progressive relaxation (get out of your mind and into your body!).

"Make sure you are sitting comfortably. Close your eyes. Gradually become aware of your body. Sit back against the chair, feet on the floor. Imagine there is a string attached to the top of your head pulling your head upwards, and in turn straightening your spine. Let your shoulders hang down and rest your hands comfortably in your lap.

"Focus on your breath. Just observe it. Let your breath come and go; there is no need to control it. You are becoming more relaxed with every breath.

"Now become aware of your scalp; allow it to relax . . . now relax your forehead . . . soften your eyeballs . . . relax your nose . . . now relax your cheeks . . . your ears . . . relax your jaw and your lips . . . relax your tongue . . . relax your neck . . . and shoulders . . . now relax your arms all the way down past your elbows, to your wrists and to your hands and fingers . . . now relax your chest and your back . . . relax your tummy . . . relax your pelvis . . . relax your legs all the way down past your knees down to your ankles, your feet and your toes . . . be aware of your whole body feeling relaxed. If you sense any tension anywhere, just put your focus back on there and allow it to relax. Enjoy this relaxed state. Enjoy feeling calm in your body. Enjoy feeling how relaxed your muscles are. Enjoy feeling calm . . . relaxed . . . peaceful.

"Take a few moments to enjoy it.

"When you are ready, start to be aware of the chair beneath you, feel the floor under your feet. Hear the sounds in the room and any coming from outside the room. Stretch or move your arms and hands, your legs and feet. When you are ready open your eyes."

- Tensing vs relaxing – the client can experience the contrast in order to know what relaxation feels like (they may not realise how tense they are).

Ask the client to tense shoulders for a few moments and then relax. Encourage them to notice the difference. Repeat several times. Try in other parts of the body.

Additional activities to suggest which can alleviate stress

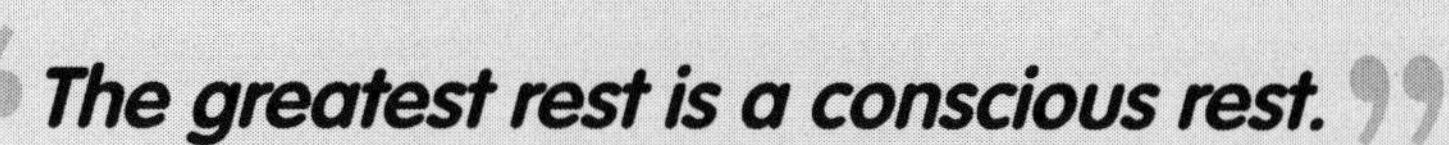

> **The greatest rest is a conscious rest.**
>
> *Meir Schneider*

From Meir Schneider, 2012, *Vision for Life: Ten Steps to Natural Eyesight Improvement.*
Reprinted by permission of North Atlantic Books.

Maximise opportunities to reduce stress as much as possible in other ways outside of therapy sessions.

- Look outside/up at the sky – appreciate the space/stillness/vastness. Appreciate the beauty.

- Expand mind – learn new things!

- Humming – "When we hear and make a repetitive sound, our brain waves slow and become similar to the delta brain waves of restorative sleep" (Barrett, 2013).

- Sound healing groups.

- Acupressure.

- Drawing, painting, mindfulness colouring books.

- Creative writing – unleash creativity.

- Write to someone you need to express yourself to – e.g. if stressed by guilt – then destroy (or send).

- Write down anything that is bothering you – and destroy.

- Emotional Freedom Technique (EFT or tapping).

- Talking.

- Aromatherapy.

- Reiki.

- Listen to (uplifting/relaxing) music – classical, new age – e.g. Alpha Music by John Levine. Try even closing your eyes and "conducting" the orchestra, hear the individual instruments – it may sound strange but can be very relaxing.

- Sing (alone or in a choir).

- Listen to guided meditation on CD/online – e.g. the many other visualisations that are available.

- Lie on a beach.

- Have a bath.

- Physical activities as listed in the chapter: "The Body, Posture and Movement".

Note: These can all be visualised if your client can't physically do it (see chapter: "The Power of the Mind").

References

Barrett, Sondra. 2013. *Secrets of Your Cells*. Boulder, CO: Sounds True Inc.

Blair, Linda. 2014. *The Key to Calm*. London: Hodder and Stoughton.

Hay, Louise L. 2004. *I Can Do It*. Carlsbad, CA: Hay House Inc.

Hibberd, Jessamy, and Usmar, Jo. 2014. *This Book Will Make You Calm*. London: Quercus.

Marshall, Lynn. 1988. *Instant Stress Cure*. London: The Leisure Circle Limited.

Moorjani, Anita. 2016. *What If This Is Heaven?* Carlsbad, CA: Hay House Inc.

Schneider, Meir. 2012. *Vision for Life: Ten Steps to Natural Eyesight Improvement*. Berkeley, CA: North Atlantic Books.

Williams, Mark and Penman, Danny. 2011. *Mindfulness*. London: Piatkus.

4. Understanding a client's experience of reality

Individual and internal

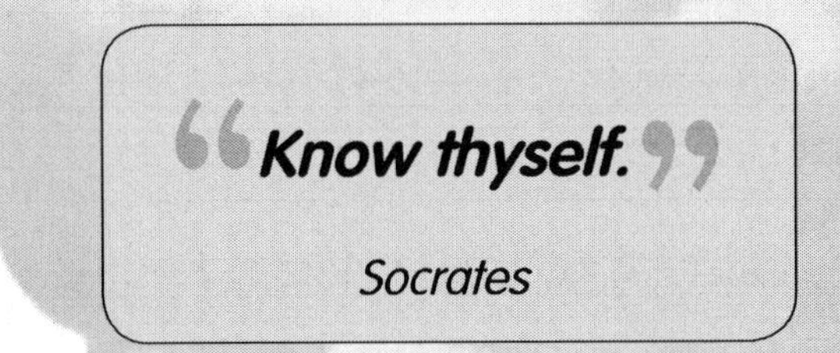

Aims

- To have a clearer understanding on what constitutes an individual's reality.

- To understand the importance and benefits of paying attention to our inner experience (our internal reality) to reduce stress and tension.

Reality

An individual's reality is their experience of life. Most people may assume reality is reality, that there is only one reality. We can however only experience our reality, or our perception of reality, our version; everybody's is unique. Even under the same conditions we would interpret and perceive a situation differently based on our conditioning (programming in childhood) and sensitivity.

Our reality is comprised of our sensory perceptions, such as what we see or hear, our thoughts and our beliefs (which come from our minds), and the feelings that result from these thoughts – emotional and physical and our awareness of our physical bodies. We think that what we perceive and process is true and accurate, hence why we hold on to our beliefs and opinions so strongly. However, our reality actually only exists inside of us and may not be the truthful representation of life as we would like to think. As

Dorothy Rowe (2003) states, "Most people grow up not understanding that all we can ever know are the meanings which we create . . . [people believe] the world *is* the way we see it." This is not the case, as our interpretation is distorted; we see through tinted glasses, coloured by our childhoods and the society we live in today. Our interpretations of and responses to a situation may be very different from our neighbour's, based on the beliefs we have inherited whilst growing up, for example from our parents and teachers. "That is why when two people look at something or someone, you get two different reactions. We see things not as they are, but as we are" (De Mello, 1990).

It may not occur to us that we can perceive things in any other way and to have a different perspective, we may even find it challenging or frightening; there is comfort and security in knowing the set order of things in our world – we understand it, and it is more predictable.

External reality

Our external reality is what occurs outside of us. In our daily lives, our minds are heavily focused on our external reality and our judgements about it. However, we cannot always control the external reality, as a result with this feeling of helplessness we are more vulnerable to being bumped along by life, and not having a sense of control.

Our attention is drawn here because we were taught to do this throughout childhood. This was necessary to learn how to adapt to the community we live in and how to conform, for survival purposes and also to avoid consequences, such as punishments.

Our internal reality was always secondary, because we had to focus on fitting in and doing what others told us to do without question. This was typically true even for very basic things: perhaps you were forced to finish everything on your plate before you could leave the table, even though inside you were experiencing discomfort because you were full. Or perhaps you had to remain standing throughout a church service even though your knees were aching. Or perhaps you were told that if you stop crying and get in the car you could have an ice cream. Also, we were led towards particular reactions based on others' reactions around us and their encouragement to think and feel similarly. We "concentrate on what we *ought* to feel, not sure of what we *actually* feel" (Rowe, 2003).

When we look back at our own childhoods we will find many more examples. The message we internalised was, ignore how you feel and instead just do what is expected of you in your external reality. We do this until we ignore or suppress our feelings and anxieties to such an extent it becomes normal, and it doesn't occur to us to lead the rest of our lives any differently. We have developed the habit of disassociating from our bodies and our inner selves.

Internal reality: our experience of life

It is ultimately inside us that we have to live and deal with, therefore as Eckhart Tolle writes in *The Power of Now* (2009), "Primary reality is within, secondary reality is without." Our internal reality is our experience of life. It comprises our minds – thoughts and beliefs and feelings – and our bodily sensations.

We are accustomed to thinking that what happens outside of us or on the physical level of our bodies is life, and this dictates how we experience our lives, but we can separate these things from our internal experience. Our usual buttons don't have to be pushed by people or situations which trigger a predictable and perhaps unpleasant reaction inside of us. They don't have to necessarily follow – you can remain calm on the inside.

Thoughts and feelings and the thinking mind

Our thinking minds *are* a significant dimension of our internal reality which gives rise to our thoughts. The mind for most of us is the main aspect of this reality because the thoughts it generates usually hijack our attention. In fact we usually assume our thoughts are us.

Thoughts appear as if out of nowhere, often they are the same old thoughts on loops, and they are fed to us non-stop for most of our waking hours. In turn they create feelings. Tension can take hold throughout the body because of our thoughts. The physical and emotional reaction is often worse than the "problem" and certainly impacts on our ability to respond to it effectively.

Thoughts, though, are just thoughts and feelings are just feelings. Just as noise is just noise. To realise they are not real or true is to realise our thoughts are akin to the pack of playing cards in *Alice in Wonderland*. Thoughts are abstract concepts; they are not tangible, they are not real. The more you focus on these the more you distance yourself and disconnect from reality – you can no longer see it as it *is* because you are not really looking and seeing, you are focused on what is in your head and therefore see only your interpretation of it.

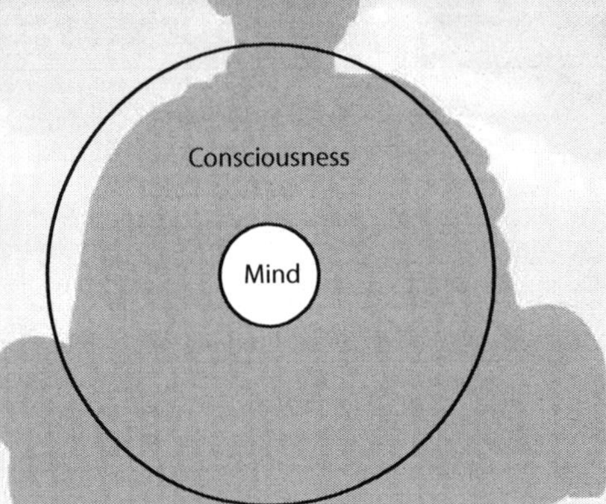

Figure 4.1 The mind within our consciousness

Thoughts typically manifest in background chatter in our heads that we are not even aware of; they tend to be negative and unhelpful – it is compulsive thinking that we become lost in. They are actually self-created dramas we are in the habit of getting preoccupied with (see chapter: "The Voice in Your Head"). They dominate our waking lives and we usually don't consciously think; thoughts happen and due to their slippery nature and ability to run away with themselves we don't usually have control over them and perhaps don't think we can.

This ceaseless chatter in our heads has the ability to cause enormous anguish and immense suffering. It fills up our heads, impeding all other productive, creative and flexible thinking.

The thinking mind is in fact only a small part of our consciousness, but most of us are not aware of this because we are in it and don't realise we can go beyond it. The mind is like a small container within our consciousness, full of our thoughts. Eckhart Tolle writes of how to go beyond the mind in *The Power of Now* (2005). He states we need to be in "no-mind", that is to quieten the mind by watching your thoughts. Wait for them to come. "Be like a cat watching a mouse hole" (Tolle, 2005). In the pauses in-between, when there are no thoughts, you are in "no-mind" when no thoughts are occurring. Normally this does happen but only rarely and we are certainly not aware of it. Another way to achieve this is by engaging fully in an activity – you are fully focused on what you are doing with no distractions from thoughts (see chapter: "An Introduction to Mindfulness for Reducing Stress"). When you are consciously in this state you are not caught up with your thoughts, and you find peace.

Our individual space

Our internal reality is a world we inhabit alone. No one can get inside our heads and think or feel for us or share what we are experiencing inside ourselves. Others may try by empathising, but no one else is really there. It can be a party of one going on inside of us, or a warm, cosy place; unfortunately more likely it is a prison or varying degrees of discomfort. Most people do not become aware of this very basic fact, do not take the time for introspection and have no real idea how the inner goings-on of our selves works. Perhaps due to the likes of Freud we are now afraid to "go there", wondering what on Earth lurks there – will I be opening a can of worms and find myself worse off? Surely you need to be prepared for years of psychoanalysis if you dare to delve? But we don't need to be so afraid. We need to take the time to learn about ourselves, to be conscious of what does happen inside of us to understand why we feel the way we do in order to improve our experience of life and manage situations more effectively. Ultimately only we can take responsibility for our own inner space.

Changing perspective through mindful awareness

Once you have the awareness that your internal reality is not always a pleasant place to be – you can see that you need to spend some time on your inner self. Look within; take the time for introspection, "[Tend] the garden of your mind" (Bolte Taylor, 2009), or as Eckhart Tolle (2005) writes, "Be the ever-alert guardian of your inner space." Make it your habit to monitor what thoughts and feelings are arising within you at any given moment, and allow yourself the opportunity to recalibrate your inner self and your nervous system – change tension to calm, the stormy seas to a mill pond.

To change and improve our primary reality for ourselves in this way we need to increase our self-awareness; develop this practice of observing ourselves – our primary reality – without judgement, and see clearly what is happening:

Observe, Observe, Observe.

If we make the effort to get into the habit of monitoring our internal state, we can free ourselves from the stress of (or at least lessen the impact) of external events – things we have less control over. Having a constant or at least frequent awareness of what is going on inside us allows us to see the reactions, understand what prompts them and realise how good we can feel if we allow ourselves to, when we don't get caught up in the storms inside. We can choose to be preoccupied with drama and know the way it will make us feel, or we can choose to avoid this and experience peace inside. It allows us to sense when we are becoming absorbed in external issues and allowing them to affect us personally and instead opt to deal with any issues whilst remaining calm on the inside.

Experiencing space and sanctuary

When you take the time to observe your mind (or the container that is your mind) and you begin to experience gaps between thoughts, you begin to become aware of the space (your consciousness that houses the mind/thoughts) that can open up inside. This space can expand to accommodate thoughts more easily. You can step away from these thoughts and be in the space instead. This space within is precious; in this nothingness is peace – it is a sanctuary, a release from the mind. There is nothing and no one. In fact it is empowering to know that you need nothing and no one to experience peace, and that it is always there, in you. It can give you the courage to look inside and see what's there, because you know if you look between and beyond the thoughts you will experience peace – in the gaps in-between thoughts. The bigger the gaps, and the bigger the space, the more peace you will experience.

Space within = Peace.

It can give clients more confidence by initially doing meditations with you, by being guided by someone they trust, by at least having someone else leading their thoughts rather than trusting their own.

Use this space and improve your inner world

Explore your inner world, unearth peace – you will find this has been forgotten because it is drowned out by the noise of the mind. *Peace is always there*. But normally, all we experience within us are self-created dramas.

We can get perpetually caught up in these dramas or experience a peaceful state of being.

We can make the choice to take the time to improve our internal world – enjoy the peace by revealing it under the layers of drama and reactions (strong emotions). We can cultivate a calm, pleasant internal reality no matter what is going on outside of us, even at the physical level of our body. We can work on feeling good and creating a happy and comfortable internal environment for ourselves. Our power lies within us, we have the power to "retreat from . . . [our] surroundings to a life of inner riches" (Frankl, 2004).

Happiness is inside us; find it by making yourself at home within.

External events/situations distract us from our first reality. If your primary focus is what is going on within you, on feeling (good), and you always bear that in mind, dramas will come and go without touching you in the same way. Through connecting with our inner selves we discover our power. We can discover inner strength, resilience and increased emotional independence. You will know then that only you can provide what you need for inner peace.

Our forgotten selves: it's ok to pay attention to ourselves

We don't realise we have a choice, because we have been conditioned to ignore our inner state, and perhaps even made to feel it is selfish or self-absorbed to reflect in this way and take the time to tend to our internal experience. Some may even hold on to their sufferings, as they have learnt it is important to suffer and it is a worthy way to live.

Clients may be more motivated to redirect their focus to prioritise tending to their internal reality if it is understood that calm and happy people are more inclined to treat others better. Also, our moods are like tuning forks – they are radiated to those around us. We have all been aware when someone who is feeling miserable or angry has managed to bring down our own mood or even made us recoil away from them. They would also have been less tuned in to the needs of those around them and likely did not respond very positively to requests. Consider also when you have been sitting in a traffic jam, late, hungry and stressed; how much less inclined were you to let someone cut in front of you, as opposed to when you were feeling relaxed? Inner peace leads to outer peace. We change the world by changing ourselves first, and change comes through taking the time to observe and understand what is happening inside.

You can free yourself from your mind.

Summary

- Our internal experience is our primary experience of life; it includes our thoughts, beliefs, feelings and bodily sensations – we have more control over these than our external reality.

- We have learnt to ignore this and focus on our external reality, believing that this is what controls our experience of life; we feel powerless on the inside and may not even see it as particularly important.

- When we realise the significance of our internal reality and our ability to improve it we can improve our experience of situations and our lives.

- We can improve our internal experience by observing our inner state as much as possible, feeling our inner bodies and understanding how we react inside to what happens outside of us, and choosing to prioritise feeling peaceful rather than getting caught up with thoughts which are causing stress and tension.

- When we can maintain a sense of calm, we are able to deal with situations more effectively.

Activities

- Reflect with the client on how we usually neglect our inner world and instead focus on the external world – even though our inner world is our real experience of life.

- Reflect on how we can make a choice to work at improving our internal state. How do they feel, and how would they prefer to feel?

- Reflect with the client on the nature of the mind – how we get caught up with the thoughts (which generates the feelings – emotional and bodily) inside of us and we then mistake them for who we are.

- Reflect on how thoughts usually just happen, and that we are not normally in control of them, but that it is possible to create and manipulate thoughts – although this can take practice.

- Reflect on how we can increase awareness of ourselves through self-observation.

- Reflect on how self-observation without judgement allows us to detach from the mind and our thoughts.

Observational activities

- Encourage the client to be aware of what they can feel inside. Do they feel like a stormy sea, or a mill pond? How big are the waves? Encourage them to feel them and watch, they need to allow time for this, and they will gradually see the waves become smaller and less choppy. It is worth doing this regularly, particularly when they are experiencing strong emotions.

- Encourage the client to think of the mind as a container – is it filled with "junk" thoughts or is it empty – peaceful? Don't try to remove the "junk", just watch it. When they are aware of what is really there, they will naturally clear it in their own time (this may take longer for some people and for some stubborn thoughts). They can also increase their awareness of how much they are getting caught up with dramas – would they prefer peace? Also encourage the client to increase the size of the container in their mind – so that the things inside have plenty of space.

- Observing the thoughts and the thinker: guided meditation for developing self-awareness.

"Make sure you are sitting comfortably. Close your eyes. Start to be aware of any thoughts that come into your mind. Do not judge them or try to change them, purely watch. Watch them as they come and go. Watch how they change from one thought and then go off on a tangent to something quite different.

"Take a few moments to do this.

"Now imagine that you are standing next to yourself whilst you are thinking. You continue to observe your thoughts and yourself, and any reactions you have to your thoughts. What sort of thoughts are they – are they worries about the past or future, or are you thinking of things you need to do today, or are you thinking of something pleasant? Be aware of the thoughts being separate from yourself – you have detached yourself from them and any reactions to them. You are the observer. You are outside of your mind and have gone beyond it. Notice how you feel. The more you can do this the less you will be affected by your thoughts, the calmer you will be and the more you will be able to act effectively."

Encourage practice of this at least once a day, and try to make this practice part of everyday situations.

- No-mind – observing the gap between thoughts.

"Make sure you are sitting comfortably. Close your eyes. Start to be aware of any thoughts that come into your mind.

"Now become very aware of the here and now, this moment – all you can hear, feel and smell. Notice the gap between your thoughts. It will probably only last a second or two to begin with as your mind is so used to ensuring it is continuously producing thoughts – it does not like nothingness or emptiness. But in that nothingness you will experience peace.

"Spend a few more moments doing this. Keep focusing on this moment and notice your thoughts being paused – even if it is just for a moment."

- Creating space/sanctuary.

"Make sure you are sitting comfortably. Close your eyes. Gradually become aware of your body. Make yourself comfortable. Sit back against the chair, feet on the floor. Imagine there is a string attached to the top of your head pulling your head upwards, and in turn straightening your spine. Let your shoulders hang down and rest your hands comfortably in your lap.

"Focus on your breath. Just observe it. Let your breath come and go; there is no need to control it.

"All your muscles are relaxing more and more. Relaxation is spreading throughout your body from your scalp and forehead, cheeks, tongue. Your eyeballs soften. Your neck, shoulders, arms, all the way past your elbows to your wrists hands and fingers. Your chest and back, your stomach, your legs all the way down past your knees to your ankles, your feet and toes. You are becoming more and more relaxed. More and more calm. If your mind wanders just gently bring your awareness back to your body.

"Now, look inside yourself. Imagine yourself as a separate, very small person within you. Imagine you are hollow inside and the little you can float all around inside. Explore – look inside your head and your body. It is completely empty, there is nothing. You are free to float. You are completely safe and free to move about however you like. You are safe and secure; no one can see you and no one can touch you here. You can hide safely from the world here; this is your sanctuary.

"Observe any colours or images you may see. Let them come and go. What is really there is nothing . . . just emptiness . . . just peace. Enjoy floating . . . enjoy this sense of peace in nothingness. You don't need anything else. You have it all within you. It is always there. This space is always within you. This peace is always in you. You can trust it is always there. You are safe inside yourself. Just remind yourself of this space, this sanctuary and you know you are in it. Take a few moments to enjoy it.

"When you are ready, start to be aware of the chair beneath you, the floor. Hear the sounds in the room and any coming from outside the room. Stretch or move your arms and hands, your legs and feet. When you are ready open your eyes."

Conscious thinking activities

- Play around with the thoughts.

"Make sure you are sitting comfortably. Close your eyes. Observe any thoughts that you have. Once you have clearly identified it, look more closely at it. Are there any images, or is it just a voice?

"If you see any images, try changing them. Just one thing at a time. Perhaps you could change the colour of something. Change the way a person looks – make them really tall, or put stilts on them. You could put a clown's nose on them, or give them hair like Rapunzel. Whatever you like. Imagine that the colours are bright. See how they move. Control how they move. Make them jump, or hop, or even do cartwheels. You can make them giggle or full-on belly laugh. Or you can imagine them completely differently. It's up to you. You can choose and control.

"If you hear any voices, play around with these. Make them shout or whisper. Make them talk in a very deep voice or high-pitched squeak. They can sing beautifully or completely off-key. They may even turn into animal noises. The more they amuse you the better. You are in control."

- Encourage the client to do this regularly to remind themselves they don't have to just be subjected to their thoughts, they can change them. This is particularly helpful when a client has a recurring negative thought.

- Encourage the client to visualise their mind as a box/container/tool box/smart phone/lap top/TV, whatever suits them, and to visualise it as a separate entity to themselves. Visualising thoughts in front of you such as on a screen can help to increase consciousness of it and to help stay outside of it, rather than being in it and consumed by it. They can switch/alternate between inner screen and external screen. They can consciously control where their focus is.

- Encourage the client to visualise filling their "container" with pleasurable things and play around with them.

References

De Mello, Anthony. 1990. *Awareness.* Grand Rapids, MI: Fount Paperbacks.

Frankl, Viktor. 2004. *Man's Search for Meaning.* London: Rider & Co.

Rowe, Dorothy. 2003. *Depression.* Hove: Routledge.

Taylor, Jill Bolte. 2009. *My Stroke of Insight.* London: Hodder & Stoughton.

Tolle, Eckhart. 2005. *The Power of Now.* London: Hodder and Stoughton Ltd.

5. The voice in your head

The voice: the antagonist within.

Aims

- To understand where the voices in our heads come from.

- To understand how we are ruled by the voices in our heads.

- To understand how the inner voice of clients can be a barrier to therapy.

- To learn how to help clients understand the voice and allow it to be without letting it affect them.

Fooled by our inner voice

The phenomenon of the unhelpful, negative and deceptive voice in the head is almost universal; according to Tolle (2006) "Almost every human body is under a great deal of strain and stress, not because it is threatened by some external factor but from within the mind."

We take the voice in our head seriously even though as Tolle (2006) writes "Every ego is the master of selective perception and distorted interpretation." We listen to it as though it is telling us important facts. We are not even usually aware of the voice in our head, but it manifests as non-stop chatter, creates our background mental atmosphere and emotions, and dictates everything we do. It holds us in a trance like state, we are at its mercy unable to escape – it is in our heads, where else do we go? How to even consider that there is an alternative version of the reality we are perceiving and interpreting? What other choice is there than to see the world through this filter?" As Sabbage (2015) writes, "We are swept away from reality by the stories we tell ourselves, then we wonder why we feel powerless and isolated and lost."

What is the voice?

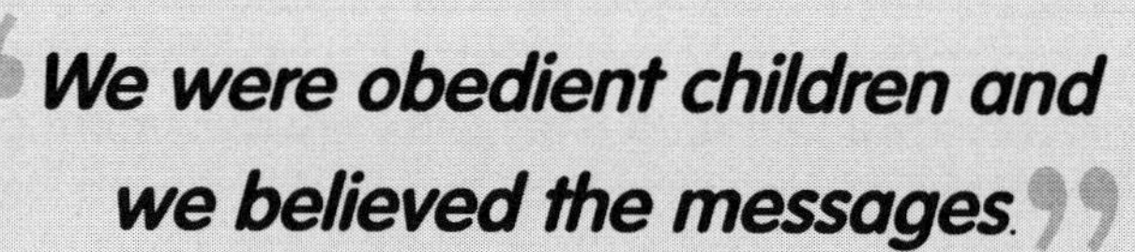

From Louise Hay, 2004, *I Can Do It*. Reprinted with permission.

The voice in our heads is not even really ours; it is the voices we heard in childhood – parents, teachers, people in the media etc. It tells you about the life you have and the situations you are in. It gives you *its* story about it, which will be distorted based upon how you have learnt to see yourself and your place in the world, therefore it will add (often quite a bit) extra – such as the "should haves".

"Are you being good for your teacher? You are extremely naughty. You are not cut out for school. Why can't you be more like . . . ? That is not good enough. What will everyone think of you if you go out like that? What on Earth are you doing? What is wrong with you?"

These are examples of spoken messages given to us, there are many more which would be unspoken. Such unquestioned inferences are *judgements* about ourselves which are internalised as we grow up.

Being judged as children = taking our freedom to be our true selves for the rest of our lives. We have been taught to live fearfully in our heads worrying about what everyone else thinks about us, being what we feel we need to be rather than just being ourselves. When we turn 18 we don't suddenly leave these judgements behind in our childhoods.

Judging in fact includes praising which according to Alfie Kohn (2005) is interpreted as love, but conditional love. ". . . the child comes to see her 'whole self' as good only when she pleases the parent. That's a powerful way of undermining self-esteem . . . [but just because] kids seem to want it [doesn't mean it's fine, rather they] take what [they] can get." Our sense of self then needs praise from others to feel "ok," conditional love given in this way becomes conditional self-approval. De Mello (1990) puts this in stronger terms – "We were brought up to need people. For what? For acceptance, approval, appreciation, applause – for what they call success. Those are words that do not correspond to reality. What is success? It is what one group of people decided is a good thing. Another group will decide the same thing is bad. . . . These are conventions. But we treat them like realities, don't we?" We come to depend on others to feed our sense of self, "Lots of people . . . [are] feeding themselves on popularity, appreciation, and praise, on 'I'm O.K., you're O.K.,' look at me, attend to me, support me, value me, on being the boss, on having power, on winning the race" (De Mello, 1990).

We are programmed to believe praise and approval are good things for children – and adults. However, "Whenever we seek approval, we are being guided from outside ourselves, and stop paying attention to what feels good. Instead of feeling what we feel, we look at the faces around us to work out what we are supposed to feel or do – and lose touch with our emotions for inner guidance. This throws us into conflict, and activates the stress response. Instead of aiming to be happy, we are trying to 'be good'" (Edwards, 2010). The "Me" I am trying to project to the world (which I have learnt to make my focus in life) has to be "good", and it is a constant internal struggle we are likely not even aware of. Also, the more we receive this praise the bigger our sense of self (ego) becomes – it feeds off praise ("Stop, you'll make his head so big he won't be able to get through the door!"). The bigger it is the more we are stuck in ourselves, the more we have to work at maintaining our sense of self, the more we stand to "lose" ("My reputation is ruined!"). Stresses will affect you more – like a larger surface area, there is more to stick to.

> If we experienced mostly praise and encouragement we will have the fear of losing that image people have come to see and of no longer doing/achieving/being enough to fit into it.

We don't think to question what we are told and the judgements that are passed as we are growing up because they come from adults who we are led to believe know best, and being so impressionable they are etched into our psyche, just another part of us; a part that we have learnt *is* us. Or they are the voices of our peers who had an increasingly strong influence during adolescence. Any bullying we experienced we also internalise, so we continue to bully ourselves long after the bullies are out of our lives.

Overcoming these voices can become a lifelong struggle for many of us as our idea of ourselves and capabilities can become set in stone – we have effectively put up mental barriers – "You have to do this", "You have to get it right", "You have to have a natural talent to do this", "You can only do this if you're good at it or everyone will laugh", "No, I can't do this", "No good at that" so that we give up even trying. We have been moulded, and as Neill (1995) writes "A lifetime of moulding is hard to break."

This voice is also known as the Critical Parent. According to Lucia Capacchione, in her book *Recovery of Your Inner Child* (1991), "The Critical Parent loves to dominate and to be the boss. . . . It likes to recite long lists of our faults, which it itemizes in detail. . . . Even if we try to please it, it finds something else to criticize. It is never satisfied. It loves to name-call, point out faults, and pick on us."

It is evident then that our inner voices are often not very helpful. They have also been referred to as "monkey mind", and it seems to have the sole purpose of winding us up at times, such as the night before an exam or interview, and a thought suddenly comes to us – "I bet you can't sleep!" Which you listen to because the voice is always taken seriously and rarely challenged, and funnily enough you don't!

The voice if left unchecked is a huge distraction because it hijacks your consciousness and absorbs so much of your thinking; it will take possession of you. You end up lost in a semi-conscious reverie, or perhaps nightmare.

Challenge the voice

Hang on a minute . . . really?

We all have these voices in our heads, but the problem lies in believing they are us rather than what they are – merely the voices we have been programmed with since small children.

Unconsciousness is the problem, lack of awareness of the unobserved mind. When we are looking the other way and not tending to our mind our thoughts take control and they are usually not constructive or pleasant. The voice in our heads does not stop, and we become lost in it. We take it to be true because we do not pay attention to it, question it and allow alternative thoughts and ideas to enter our minds. This is of course not helped by the fact we are not ordinarily encouraged to question or challenge anything as we grow up.

To become free of the negative effects of our inner voice we first need to get in the habit of catching ourselves whilst thinking – be aware of our thoughts and subsequent emotions as they are happening. Once you do that you automatically separate from them – they are not you, and you will see them more clearly, often as grossly exaggerated half-truths, or even completely absurd. You are not denying them, you are allowing them to be, but they won't have the same power over you. Eckhart Tolle (2006) describes it as ". . . the shift from thinking to awareness."

Revealing your inner voice and holding it under the spotlight ". . . is to expose it for what it is: an emperor with no clothes, a dictator with no power. It only has as much power as we give it" (Capacchione, 1991). Once you are aware of your thoughts you will also be able to engage in "voice management" as Gill Edwards (2010) describes it – that is choosing the voices in your head ". . . wisely and consciously." According to Jill Bolte Taylor (2009) ". . . paying attention to our-self talk is vitally important for our mental health . . . making the decision that internal verbal abuse is not acceptable behavior, is the first step toward finding deep inner peace."

Lucia Capacchione also recommends balancing negative voices in our heads by making a conscious effort to bring out your inner "nurturing" and "protective parent". She also suggests encouraging your inner "assertive child" to stand up to the inner critic.

The key point is to step outside who you think you are and not let your thoughts take over "you". The voice is always inside us not out there in reality. It is the storyteller in our head, not "you". "You" wouldn't choose to make up those stories, would you? There is no need to take them seriously.

This is freedom, no longer being controlled by the voice in our head.

Who am I – letting go of thoughts and beliefs

Return to yourself – rediscover yourself.

If we are not who we thought (a bundle of thoughts that come and go), then who are we? For this we step outside and go beyond the mind, to find the observing presence discussed in the chapter *Introduction to Mindfulness*. This is our essence, not the content of our lives, and it is beyond words. It is ". . . the life that you are [not] the life that you have, or seem to have . . . [which are actually just thoughts and so are part of the] experience [in the moment], not the experiencer . . . who is prior to all experience but without whom there would be no experience" (Tolle, 2006). You will find there a different intelligence, and you will find strength, space, peace and the joy of being. This dimension is ordinarily obscured.

Our observing self (unconditioned consciousness/awareness) can be experienced through mindfulness – becoming aware of the space, or container in which thoughts occur so that you can see there *is* an outside to retreat to, and which can be a permanent sanctuary. "If you can sense an alert inner stillness in the background whilst things happen in the foreground – that's it!" (Tolle, 2006) You will be making room in your consciousness for something other than your thinking mind.

Stepping aside from thoughts involves letting go, or at least clinging less tightly to our ideas, words, labels, beliefs, and illusions about ourselves – and not trying to think about and protect "me". Awareness is not part of thinking. Words can't explain who we are, we don't need to define ourselves, we can just "be." In fact it is liberating not to worry about trying to be something or someone in particular, and not knowing – "Who are you?" "I don't know!" Separate the real "you" from the thought version. Allowing ourselves to be free of the prison of labels, instead we are something that has scope for exploration. Instead of thinking "I can't do that", this can now be turned around to "I don't know, maybe I can, I will give it a go and see." Let go of beliefs and free yourself! Unlearn. Challenge your beliefs. Is it true? Question everything. As Socrates said, "The only true wisdom is in knowing you know nothing." Things will not bother you in the same way when you simply observe yourself without judgement. You can get on with dealing with situations, not mind-made stories (problems).

The voice and mindfulness

Focus on life, not just the commentary.

By being mindful we can observe, understand and respect all inner voices instead of judging or fighting them. We can accept the (inevitable) negative voices in our heads, we can allow them and the subsequent emotional response to come and go and as Tolle (2005) writes "One day you may catch yourself smiling at the voice in your head, as you would smile at the antics of a child. This means that you no longer take the content of your mind all that seriously . . ."

As you grow in awareness of the voices you become quieter and more peaceful on the inside which allows you to be in life, in reality, and not holed up in your head living a less pleasant version.

Being mindful quietens the voice; it provides a respite from it.

> **"*Stop thinking, and end your problems.*"**
>
> *Lao Tzu*

The voice and clients

Through talking with your client about our inner voices – which we all have – they can begin to become aware of it in themselves, accept it and challenge what it is saying. Without the (inner) voice holding the client back so much they will be able to let go of fears and concerns and be able to participate fully in therapy.

You can simply talk about the "inner voice" in general terms, as something everyone has, e.g. "Everyone has a voice or voices in their head which are usually very critical and harsh. It is the voices of the adults we grew up with. As children we are taught to be obedient and do the 'right thing'. So the voice continues to get on to us about doing things 'right'. It's not very forgiving." Talking about it in a broad way like this, your client is able to acknowledge this in themselves if they choose, but they can understand that you are saying it not directly about them, you are saying it because you can assume everyone is the same. It does not have to go any deeper than that – just mentioning the inner voice and allowing the client to understand. They may then feel that that might be the case for others but not for them, but they may acknowledge it later, when they have taken time for contemplation. It is a personal thing that can help them, and does not need to be verbally acknowledged, but in my experience it usually is and it can be a relief to know they are not the only ones.

Summary

- Everyone experiences the voices in their head. These are the voices from our past.

- These voices tell stories about our lives and pass judgements.

- They are often critical and unhelpful and create fear in us.

- These voices are allowed to fill our consciousness (with negative thoughts and feelings), are accepted as true and dictate our lives if we do not observe them and are not conscious of them.

Activities

- Take a few minutes to allow the client to listen to the voice in their head. Encourage them to take the time to see what it is saying, how negative/unhelpful/unsupportive it is, how many thoughts are on a loop – being played repeatedly without being able to move on or benefit from them in any way. You can suggest your client write down all these worrying thoughts – getting them down on paper can help clients to see that there are just a few playing on a loop (you don't need to see them, and is probably best you state clearly that you won't look at them to allow the client to write freely). Encourage the client to question if what the voice is saying is true – how much drama has been added, how much dwelling is going on of situations that have never happened and never likely to happen? Whose voice does it sound like e.g. a parent? Encourage your client to challenge the voice and see it for the negative irritation it is rather than accepting it for the gospel truth.

- Encourage your client to change the (inner) voice – play around with it. Russ Harris (2007) in his book *The Happiness Trap* recommends making the voice say the usual things but in a different pitch or a cartoon character's voice. Allow the client to feel some control over it whilst adding a bit of humour – this will help burst the bubble – for the voice to release the client from its total control. They can then try adding another voice to make a dialogue rather than a monologue – the second voice can challenge the original voice, perhaps point out the absurdities.

- Encouraging your client to talk to themselves out loud will help increase awareness of what the voice is actually saying.

- Doing the activities suggested in the chapter *Introduction to Mindfulness* can also help your client to quieten the voice in their head by connecting with reality directly instead, rather than through the voice's distorted version.

References

Capacchione, Lucia. 1991. *Recovery of Your Inner Child*. New York, NY: Simon and Schuster.

De Mello, Anthony. 1990. *Awareness*. Grand Rapids, MI: Fount Paperbacks.

Edwards, Gill. 2010. *Conscious Medicine*. London: Little, Brown Book Group.

Harris, Russ. 2007. *The Happiness Trap*. London: Robinson Publishing Ltd.

Hay, Louise L. 2004. *I Can Do It*. Carlsbad, CA: Hay House Inc.

Kohn, Alfie. 2005. *Unconditional Parenting*. New York, NY: Atria Books.

Neill, A.S. 1995. *Summerhill School*. New York, NY: St. Martin's Griffin.

Sabbage, Sophie. 2015. *The Cancer Whisperer*. London: Coronet.

Taylor, Jill Bolte. 2009. *My Stroke of Insight*. London: Hodder & Stoughton.

Tolle, Eckhart. 2005. *The Power of Now*. London: Hodder and Stoughton.

Tolle, Eckhart. 2006. *A New Earth*. London: Penguin Books.

6. An introduction to mindfulness for reducing stress

Change your perspective – from being yourself, to observing yourself.

Aims

- To understand what mindfulness is.

- To learn how observing and detaching from thoughts, and instead connecting directly with all that is in reality can shift our perspective on our lives and our situations and lower stress levels.

What is mindfulness?

Mindfulness is consciously taking in what is going on within you (internal reality) and outside of you (external reality). It is observing and attending consciously and with curiosity to what is going on right here, in the present moment, moment by moment, so that you see and experience life directly through the senses, without words and without judgement. Normally we see life in terms of our words, labels and concepts – preconceived ideas and prejudices which limit our ability to fully perceive situations accurately, as De Mello (1990) states,

> Are you imprisoned by your concepts? Do you want to break out of your prison? Then look; observe. . . . Hopefully you will then break out of these rigid patterns we have all developed, out of what our thoughts and words have imposed on us. Hopefully we will see. What will we see? This thing we choose to call reality, whatever is beyond words and concepts. . . . What I'm leading you to is awareness or reality around you. Awareness means to watch, to observe what is going on within you and around you.

Words are generated in our minds to aid thinking and explore concepts; they are symbols representing the real thing. But "Words cannot give you reality. They only point, they only indicate" (De Mello, 1990). They become a distraction, as they are never the thing themselves and end up becoming a barrier to reality. We get caught up with labels and judgements which cloud our vision of the here and now, and so we may never really see what is before us. The problem arises because we are not aware of this and the fact that we live through them – that is through our stories (in our minds) or "interpretation of experience rather than the experience itself" (Rome, 2014). It is as though our thoughts are more real than reality, as Michael Neill (2016) writes,

> We live in a world of thought, but we think we live in a world of external experience . . . we [actually] live in a world of unrecognized thought. Thought is the architect of both hope and despair, the source of every color in the emotional rainbow. Without thought, there would be no delineation in our [personal] world[s], like the pure clarity of light before it passes through a prism and bursts into a kaleidoscope of color. But unrecognized thought demands our attention and fills our consciousness.

> *"There is nothing either good or bad, but thinking makes it so."*
>
> William Shakespeare, *Hamlet*

When we can appreciate the benefits of seeing past words and our ideas and beliefs and breaking through the confines of the mind, we can truly experience reality (internal and external), as it is, not masked and distorted by our internal chattering mind. All you have to do is be fully in the present moment, attend, observe, experience and accept what "is" directly. This will centre you and anchor you and allow you clarity of mind. You will have the ability to meet challenges as situations to tackle rather than stresses, and you will experience the joy of being. The benefits of mindfulness are not anecdotal; mindfulness has been proven by science to have "multiple physiological as well as psychological benefits . . . including stress reduction, cardiovascular health, improved mood, and increased emotional intelligence" (Rome, 2014).

Observe   Experience without Judgement   Accept

It sounds simple, but we find it extremely challenging to do just this – typically we can't interact with reality without judging, comparing and analysing. Our analytical left hemisphere is the dominant (and vocal) one, and it is a huge barrier to experiencing life as it actually is.

> **It's not that there isn't a world 'out there,' but that our experience of it is 100% an experience of our own thinking.**
>
> *Michael Neill*

From Michael Neill, 2016, *The Space Within*. Reprinted with permission.

Because of this automatic response to analyse we instantly make decisions about things (based on our programming), which also affect our ability to see things clearly, without distortion or bias. We jump in feet first without taking the time to really see and understand. "Change your exclamation mark for a question mark" (Kohn, 2005) and you will approach life and its challenges with curiosity, something that can be explored and figured out rather than something you feel burdened with.

You simply need to observe to increase your awareness of yourself. Look at your thoughts and emotions but also see beyond them, rather than getting completely distracted by them and the world around you. With increased awareness, understanding and detachment you will notice your life improves as you act differently. The moment will guide you if you fully experience it – because you will understand the situation. As you drop your concepts and delusions, you will also experience more peace and joy because you have dropped the barriers to these positive states of being which lie masked underneath, "You become happy by contact with reality. That's what brings happiness, a moment by moment contact with reality. . . . What I'm leading you to is awareness of reality around you. Awareness means to watch, to observe what is going on within you and around you" (De Mello, 1990).

> **"Watch your thoughts,**
> **hey become words.**
> **Watch your words,**
> **They become actions.**
> **Watch your actions,**
> **They become habits.**
> **Watch your habits,**
> **They become character.**
> **Watch your character,**
> **It becomes your destiny."**
>
> *Lao Tzu*

Normal mode: autopilot

Habits: mindless routine activities which dominate most of our daily lives. We are not fully conscious, not present, not fully attending, not noticing all that makes up life. For most of our lives we are existing and operating like automatons.

Our lives are typically a series of routines and habits – and a bit like the film *Groundhog Day*. We know where we are, where we're going, what we're doing – it's all ok – everything is as usual, and we tick along, perhaps feeling ok about that or perhaps feeling it is all a drudgery, but that's life, isn't it?

We interact with niceties such as "How are you?" not really expecting a full and complete answer, only the standard, "Fine, thank you. And you?" Box ticked, performance carried out as expected by all parties. Or when we talk to young children, we may respond typically with either "Good boy!" or "If you don't stop doing that right now I am going to get really angry with you!" Not really ever taking the time to think if there is an alternative more respectful or constructive response that allows you to connect on a deeper level with the child and be fully with them – and even enjoy them more. It would be especially hard to do if you have things to achieve, a long "to do" list and the child is preventing you from doing this in the timeframe you had in your mind. Your priority and therefore your attention is on the goal and all that it is demanding of you, not the here and now.

Life can become a box-ticking exercise. We become so attached to satisfying ourselves that we are ticking these boxes that the preoccupation with this becomes our experience of life, to the point that we miss out on it.

> **If you are depressed, you are living in the past.**
> **If you are anxious, you are living in the future.**
> **If you are at peace, you are living in the present.**
>
> *Lao Tzu*

Where or when are you really?

Being absorbed with our endless thinking and analyses involves constantly referring back to/regretting past events and anticipating/worrying about future ones. But the past and future do not exist except in our own minds. Only this moment can ever be happening right now, so "When we are hooked into cognitive thoughts and running mental loops, technically we are not in the present moment" (Bolte Taylor, 2009). It is only in the now that we are living and that we have any control over. As De Mello urges (1990),

> Get into today. Someone said, "Life is something that happens to us while we're busy making other plans". . . . Live in the present moment. This is one of the things you will notice happening to you as you come awake. You find yourself living in the present, tasting every moment as you live it.

You can live the life you actually have or your attention can be tied up somewhere else, in another time. You do have a choice, but you need to be *conscious* of this tendency in order to be in control of where and when you are.

Resistance to the Now/What Is

What makes us unhappy is comparing reality with how we think it should be.

Being present in the moment (mindful/conscious) will initially be harder if you don't feel you like now as it is. You will naturally try to pull away, not be near it, let alone *in* it, and perhaps even bury your head completely (we may reduce our levels of consciousness and avoid reality through alcohol, drugs, TV etc.). But as Eckhart Tolle in *The Power of Now* (2005) discusses, it is not "life" (right here and now as such) that you are resisting but your "life situation". Your "life" is real and your "life situation" is mind-stuff, abstraction, the stories you tell yourself about your situation, as the Dalai Lama states in *The Art of Happiness* (1999), "all afflictive emotions and thoughts, are essentially distorted, in that they are rooted in misperceiving the actual reality of the situation."

Your situation – what is going on in and around you is not how you would like it to be, but it is your comparing that is the problem. How you perceive it to be versus what you think it should be (which involves projecting yourself to a different time and place to consider how it was and perhaps comparing with what others might have, what you could have and what you think you should have based on preconceived ideas that you are unwilling to let go of). It is the distance between what you want and how you think it is which leads to unease in your mind and tension in your body.

If it is your preconceived ideas that are causing turmoil and resistance to what is, then it is worth questioning if these ideas are even true. We are accustomed to taking our thoughts as accurate facts, but we now know they are not always and as such cannot be trusted. For example a father with young children may have the unchallenged assumptions that having children should bring you closer to your partner, or that you need to go on dates in order to keep a relationship fresh. Are these really true though? Without being aware that he holds these ideas he is at risk of feeling discontentment when the reality for him does not match. These are examples of our expectations about what "should happen" which will allow us to be "happy", but as Tolle (2006) writes,

Don't seek happiness. If you seek it, you won't find it, because seeking is the antithesis of happiness. Happiness is ever elusive, but freedom from unhappiness is attainable now, by facing what is rather than making up stories about it.

Why are you battling life? It is what it is

Challenges that arise are to be dealt with or left alone, but it is only the mind that makes them "problems" – "Why make anything into a problem? Isn't life challenging enough as it is? What do you need problems for?" (Tolle, 2005). You can choose to connect with the reality of life or unconsciously create an alternative and less pleasant version of reality in your mind, which then becomes your identity. Strangely enough we try to cling to this identity – for who are we if we are not the person we have told ourselves we are? That can be scary.

It is a struggle maintaining this false sense of reality. Due to the negativity associated with it and also because of the falseness of it; it is stressful and draining. You can wake up and connect with reality.

Understanding and acceptance: waking up to reality

"Ah, so THIS is life!"

Reality is what it is and it is the fighting with it that causes the problems. As Byron Katie (2002) writes, "The reason I made friends . . . with reality – is that I discovered it's quite insane to oppose it. When I argue with reality, I lose – but only 100% of the time." It is our expectations that create the problems. To go with the flow of life we cannot have expectations, we just have to allow for our ever-changing reality and see what it brings with curiosity, not judgement.

When you come to this realisation, by being in and accepting the here and now you can give up your battle, you can choose to stop the struggle and instead surrender. Past and future, and "what ifs" and "if onlys", are not relevant.

This is what it is to be human. Be curious about the experience.

Figure 6.1 The flow of life

You can see it for the journey that it is, that you happen to be on. You can value it for what it is rather than lamenting it for what it is not. You can enjoy taking in all the curious aspects of it. You can also move on and redirect your attention to dealing with situations in a more effective way without distraction (for more on acceptance, see chapter: "Acceptance, Appreciation and Moving On").

Be led by life.

How to be mindful

When you are mindful and go beyond the analytical mind you become the observing presence that is pure consciousness. Watch as a detached bystander, like when you are people-watching or watching a film. You observe and allow the scene to play out without trying to do anything, as "You are the observer, nothing more" (Kinslow, 2014).

To be mindful you need to attend to all that is happening outside of you – or rather what you perceive through your senses – sights, sounds, tactile sensations, smells and tastes. But not just vaguely aware of them – you need to be fully experiencing them, to magnify the moment. Take your attention away from your thinking mind to the life that is really happening to you. When you start to do this you realise how much of your life you have been missing.

At the same time you also need to be aware of what is happening within you, in your body and your mind. Notice any thoughts, and allow and accept them in a detached way. When you do this they will gradually disappear, "And when this occurs, an extraordinary thing can happen: a profound sense of happiness and peace fills the void" (Williams and Penman, 2011). This is also the space where true insight comes, which can be profound and allow you to see situations in a whole new way (see also chapter: "Understanding a Client's Experience of Reality").

If you are feeling negative, be aware of that, allow it to be and pass as you consciously focus on it, but know when you are fully mindful, there is no judgement to create negativity in the first place.

It doesn't matter what you feel or observe – just be aware of it and fully accept what *is* and then stay with it. See what is there both inside (thoughts, emotions and bodily sensations) and outside the self with a curious mind rather than with fear. In *Your Body Knows the Answer* (2014), David I. Rome also calls this "friendly attending."

Curiosity not fear.

You need to accept any thoughts or physical reactions you have to the point that it doesn't matter if they are there or not. When you see the mostly unsolicited thoughts as just self-created dramas, not real or tangible things (like a holographic image) which generate your feelings and emotions, they will release you.

You really don't need to worry about them. Allow them to come, and go, as they always do.

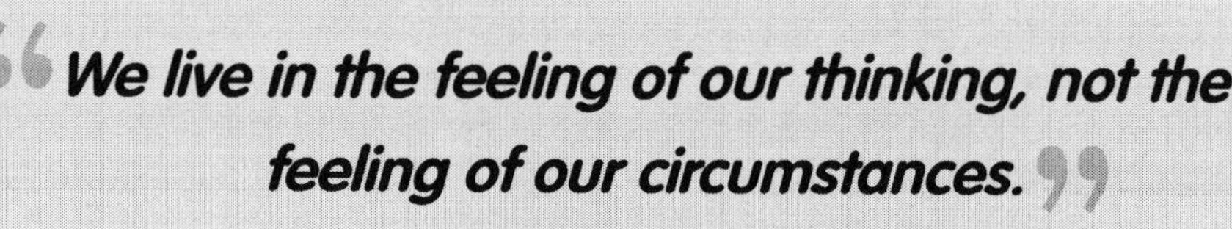

From Michael Neill, 2016, *The Space Within*. Reprinted with permission.

It takes courage to confront a situation in which you are not comfortable, but that is just what you need to do. You need to turn toward all you can experience in the here and now, both within you and without, even if "unpleasant". It is not your job to do anything indeed it is unlikely to be helpful. "[Feelings/states of mind and body] are not problems to be solved. They are emotions. . . . As such, they cannot be *solved* – only *felt*" (Williams and Penman, 2011). Stay with them and allow them to be and change on their own as you give them your full attention.

Feel   Listen   Observe   Accept   Trust   =   FLOAT

Shining the light of awareness

Look and see.

Through observing and realising you are the observer, you can step outside of your mind and yourself where your stagnant, repetitive thoughts occur and you can create distance between you and them.

Just realise you are thinking – catch yourself when you are in the middle of a thought. Just being aware like this bursts the bubble and releases you from the thought – you are now outside of it, you can see it is just a thought. You are now back in the here and now.

Consider – are you in the thought or looking in at it? A thought is like a vortex, it has a powerful pull and we get sucked in. Staying out of the thought, and being conscious of having the thought in real time – that is, as you are having it – is what David Rome describes as "meta-awareness, in which we are aware that we are aware or rather conscious of having a thought. . . . This enhances mental clarity and gives rise to more vivid perceptions and penetrating insights into the true nature of things" (Rome, 2014). With this distance you can reduce or take away the emotional pain that goes with them, because you can clearly see they are not "you" and can keep them at arm's length if you choose.

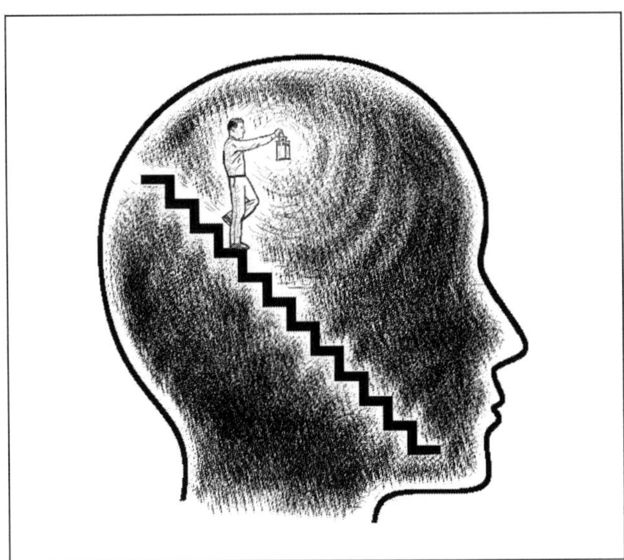

Figure 6.2 The light of awareness

"To watch everything in you and around you as far as possible and watch it as if it
were happening to someone else. . . . It means that you do not personalize what
is happening to you. It means you look at things as if you have no connection
whatsoever with no comment, no judgement, no attitude, no interference, no
attempt to change, only to understand. As you do this you'll begin to realize that
increasingly you are disidentifying from "me".

(De Mello, 1990)

To watch yourself in this way, in fact, is to observe human nature and see how we are
programmed by others during our formative years, therefore it cannot be personal.

Your consciousness is the container that holds and allows for all your experiences, you
just need to be aware of it. You can contain all that you are experiencing. You are either
observing on the outside, aware that you are bigger than it and any emotions that are there,
or you are in it, and liable to feeling engulfed by all that is going on inside and outside of you
and vulnerable to feeling overwhelmed. This shift in perspective and the space it gives you is
very powerful, and you will be able to see your life situation differently as you take away the
pressure, expectation, any resistance and the ongoing struggle to change reality.

Consciously separate, detach from your mind, your thoughts, emotions, sensations,
including pain, fatigue, fuzzy headedness, boredom, stress and tension (e.g. I am not
tense, tension is there), but also "pleasurable" thoughts and feelings. See them as
separate to "you", like separate entities within, that exist within parts of you but are not
"you". Be the impartial observer of all that is being experienced within you – then expand
your consciousness to include all that is outside as well as inside you. Increase your
awareness of all that is in the here and now, such as the other people you are with, and
the space that is the room you are in. You can expand your consciousness further to
increase your awareness of the street you are on, the town, the country, the planet, the
solar system, the universe, and the space that contains them all. With such awareness
thoughts and emotions do not consume all of you – you realise you have space that can

Figure 6.3 A thought machine – a person doesn't realise they can move away from it

expand and make room for all that is (this is "meta-meta-awareness . . . like the vast open space of consciousness", Rome, 2014, *Your Body Knows the Answer*). You are now outside your head, outside your mind, and experience any tension and thoughts from a different perspective, a clearer vantage point.

Expanding your awareness of this space within and without allows you to perceive and accommodate all aspects of reality as it is ("good" and "bad"); it separates you from emotions/reactions. You see things much more clearly and you will feel calm and in control in this ever-present space. You still allow emotions to be, but you can respond in a more appropriate and constructive way. Think of it as not "your" life, but a life you have been given to observe from this space of awareness. By being present in this moment, being conscious you will find space.

You are simply watching and allowing everything – including the thoughts/the mind/"me".

Through mindfulness, then, you do not conquer your mind, instead you become conscious of it at work, i.e. your thoughts. "Consciousness is the gift of awareness" (Neill, 2016), awareness of our thoughts and the ability to "look past the illusion of our own thinking" which is genuinely not you, but merely appears so. There is then no need to battle, to try is only to lose. When you begin to observe thoughts you will realise how relentless they are, and it is only through conscious observation of them that they can begin to settle. Peace of mind is thus a by-product of consciousness, not the goal. The aim is to do this this as much as possible – to be fully awake throughout our waking hours.

> *The moment we remember that we are not our thinking, we are the space where thoughts arise, we can experience the storm with the awe of an arctic explorer seeing the aurora borealis, with the delight of the sailor watching the liquid dance of St. Elmo's fire, or with the impartiality of the sky. When the storm has run its course, we'll continue on our way, unaffected by the content of our thinking but deeply touched by the gift of Thought, the Consciousness that allows us to experience it, and the ever-present Mind inside which life continues to unfold.*
>
> *Michael Neill*

From Michael Neill, 2016, *The Space Within*. Reprinted with permission.

Wake up to the world around you

Realise you are observing the here and now.

If you go through the day observing everything with care as though experiencing it all for the first time, and don't assume every leaf or every stone is the same, and you let go of the feeling that you have "seen it all", you "know it", and you are open to all that life is right now, you will begin to cultivate awe and wonder. If you are aware of the wonders of life you can begin to awaken to the miracle of mindfulness, you will awaken to the miracle of life. Everyday life can then be a joy rather than a slog and a grind.

It is like reading a book to a small child for the hundredth time – they are enjoying the pictures and the story, and you just get the printed word form which you have stopped really seeing. You can take the time to enjoy the full colour of the pictures – and you can take the time to enjoy all the colours of life! Life can be experienced in all its Technicolor glory – vivid, crisp, sharp and clear. You need to take the time to feel it in order to appreciate it, know it and understand.

Be interested in everything in you and around you. Expand your awareness beyond the thinking mind. Be curious. Be open to the moment. What are the possibilities in this moment?

Benefits of mindfulness for clients/how mindfulness can help clients achieve therapy goals

"Learning to listen to your brain from the position of a non-judgmental witness may take some practice and patience, but once you master this awareness, you become free to step beyond the worrisome drama and trauma of your story-teller" (Bolte Taylor, 2009). Mindfulness frees clients from the concerns and worries which exacerbate tension and allows them to be fully present in therapy sessions – to participate to their full potential and gain maximum benefits. It will also help clients to accept their situation and let go of the thoughts that preoccupy them. Their attention will be more readily drawn to you and what you are trying to do with them instead of the futile, demoralising battle they have going on inside them.

Clients will feel more confident and at ease in themselves, as they will have increased confidence to manage their thoughts and feelings rather than feeling overpowered by them. They will know that they are not their thoughts. This can also be an opportunity for clients to discover life in a way they never knew they could, a more peaceful life, in which they are safe to explore themselves and their potential.

This moment, it is all we have – it's an opportunity/space in which we create our lives.

Experience, explore and create.
Life is but a series of moments.

Summary

- Mindfulness is sustained conscious attention to all that is in the here and now – in the experience available to us in the moment (our thoughts, emotions and bodily sensations, and all that happens outside ourselves).

- Curiosity, non-judgement and acceptance are the key characteristics.

- Mindfulness helps to reduce stress by increasing and expanding our awareness – of our minds and thoughts, and all that is beyond them, so that our thoughts do not completely fill our consciousness and consume us, and we can then see life more clearly from a better vantage point.

- Mindfulness helps to change our perspective by seeing that we can detach from everything we experience (including our thoughts and feelings), but being more aware of it so that we are in a better space to respond more effectively in situations.

- Inner peace is a by-product of detached observation, as judgement (and thereby pressure) is removed.

Activities

(See also chapters: "Understanding a Client's Experience of Reality" and "The Breath" for more activities.)

- Discuss mindfulness with your client. Encourage the client to regularly remind themselves that the thought they are having is just a thought and they just need to be aware of it. Everyone has unpleasant thoughts; they are no different. But they don't need to judge them or feel responsible for them, all they need to do is be aware of them and stay with them until they go. If they fight the thoughts, they will stay longer.

- If the client verbalises a specific thought which you see as being a product of conditioning or past experience, e.g. "I can never think of anything sensible to say." Try to guide them through to help them realise it is not necessarily true, with specific questions such as "Why do you think that?" Is that really true in all situations?" "Can you think of a time when you felt you were communicating well?" "Who were you with?" What were you talking about?"

- Visualise sitting alone in a desert on a starry night. Imagine all this space outside of you is your mind. See any thoughts within this expanded mind as small and just in front of you. Watch any thoughts and be aware of the space. You can still be out of your head whilst still in your mind.

- Encourage the client to step outside themselves, and view themselves as a separate person, to depersonalise their experience.

- Encourage the client to make changes to their routine and do things differently sometimes, like walking around the house barefoot if they normally wear socks.

- Encourage the client to relax into the now.

- Encourage the client to be aware of how they are feeling when they are doing any activities. How do they really feel? Do they really like it? Encourage them to really question this particularly when doing things they usually like, such as watching a film, knitting or doing a puzzle. Are they feeling good throughout the activity? Notice any changes. Often things we really like doing can end up having a compulsive element to them so that you don't feel you can stop even if you have gone beyond the point of enjoyment.

- Encourage the client to "people-watch" and observe their judgements of them. It is helpful to increase their awareness of their judgements, particularly to understand the frequency and harshness/severity of them.

- Encourage the client to always be aware of the "pull" towards being in the mind and getting caught up with worries and the past and future. They need to pull themselves back towards reality in the here and now. Encourage them to be the observer of their thoughts as much as possible. If thoughts are different to how they are feeling, it is our feelings that reflect accurately what is happening inside of us – we can try to fool ourselves with our thoughts. In that case feelings will need more attention and understanding.

Guided meditations

- "Close your eyes, and allow yourself to begin to relax. Become aware of your body and breath. Focus on each part of you, one at a time. Feel yourself become more and more relaxed, more and more calm.

  "Is there a problem right now? Is it really a problem? Is it right here, right now?"

- "Close your eyes, and allow yourself to begin to relax. Become aware of your body and breath. Focus on each part of you, one at a time. Feel yourself become more and more relaxed, more and more calm.

  "Watch your thoughts and feelings inside you. How are you feeling? Your inner self is talking to you all the time, take the time to listen. Your mind and body are the messengers and your thoughts and feelings are the messages. They may be telling you about something in your life or something you are doing that needs to change. Take the time to practise listening now. If any feeling is unpleasant – stay with it. I am with you as you are experiencing it. If you give it enough time it will get easier, it will release its hold on you. If your mind wanders that's fine, just watch it – what are you thinking? And then gently bring it back to awareness of what you are feeling now. You really don't need to worry about what you're thinking. You have been programmed throughout your life to judge, but you don't need to, it's not helpful right now. Just allow your experience to be, be aware of it and see what happens.

  "Do this as much as possible throughout the day. You need to know what is happening inside of you, it is your life, it is your experience of life."

- "Close your eyes, and allow yourself to begin to relax. Become aware of your body and breath. Focus on each part of you, one at a time. Feel yourself become more and more relaxed, more and more calm.

  "Feel every part of you – your scalp . . . your forehead . . . your eyes . . . your nose . . . your lips . . . your tongue . . . your jaw . . . your neck . . . your shoulders . . . your chest . . . your back . . . your arms . . . your hands . . . your fingers . . . your tummy . . . your pelvis . . . your legs . . . your feet . . . your toes. Notice any sensations you have, just watch them, it doesn't matter what they are, just feel. Be aware of the whole of you. Be very aware you are inside your body; this is the vehicle you inhabit. Feel it. Enjoy the feeling. Enjoy feeling calm. Take a few more moments to be fully in your body.

  "When you are ready, in your own time you can start to be aware of the chair you are sitting on, perhaps stretch as you feel you want to, and then open your eyes."

Note: You can also just focus on the hands and feet to start with. It can be easier to connect with and feel more in control of extremities. Encourage the client to be aware of the tension there and release it.

- "Close your eyes, and allow yourself to begin to relax. Become aware of your body and breath. Focus on each part of you, one at a time. Feel yourself become more and more relaxed, more and more calm.

"Now watch your thoughts going round in your mind. Imagine they are in your washing machine. Be aware of what is in there but allow them to be churned around in the washing machine. The machine will turn off when it is ready. You find it's getting a bit boring watching the same old thoughts going round so you can start to focus on your body again while that is going on (your thoughts are being dealt with now). You can now come out of your mind and go into your body. Feel every part of you – your scalp . . . your forehead . . . your eyes . . . your nose . . . your lips . . . your tongue . . . your jaw . . . your neck . . . your shoulders . . . your chest . . . your back . . . your arms . . . your hands . . . your fingers . . . your tummy . . . your pelvis . . . your legs . . . your feet . . . your toes. Notice any sensations you have, just watch them, it doesn't matter what they are, just feel. Be aware of the whole of you. Be very aware you are inside your body; this is the vehicle you inhabit. Feel it. Enjoy the feeling. Enjoy feeling calm. Take a few more moments to be fully in your body.

"When you are ready, in your own time you can start to be aware of the chair you are sitting on, perhaps stretch as you feel you want to, and then open your eyes."

References

De Mello, Anthony. 1990. *Awareness*. Grand Rapids, MI: Fount Paperbacks.

HH Dalai Lama and Cutler, Howard C. 1999. *The Art of Happiness*. New York: Penguin.

Katie, Byron. 2002. *Loving What Is*. London: Rider Books.

Kinslow, Frank J. 2014. *When Nothing Works Try Doing Nothing*. Sarasota, FL: Lucid Sea.

Kohn, Alfie. 2005. *Unconditional Parenting*. New York, NY: Atria Books.

Neill, Michael. 2016. *The Space Within*. London: Hay House.

Rome, David I. 2014. *Your Body Knows the Answer*. Boston, MA: Shambhala Publications Inc.

Taylor, Jill Bolte. 2009. *My Stroke of Insight*. London: Hodder & Stoughton.

Tolle, Eckhart. 2005. *The Power of Now*. London: Hodder & Stoughton.

Tolle, Eckhart. 2006. *A New Earth*. London: Penguin Books.

Williams, Mark and Penman, Danny. 2011. *Mindfulness*. London: Piatkus.

7. Meditation

Our attempts to do anything are likely to be more successful when we are experiencing a quiet and peaceful state of mind.

Aims

- To learn about what meditation is.

- To learn about the benefits of clients practising meditation in therapy sessions, and continuing independently outside of therapy.

What is it?

According to Madonna Gauding in *The Meditation Bible* (2005), meditation is "simply making a choice to focus your mind on something". Everything you do is a form of meditation – even preparing dinner. "The question is, what are you choosing to meditate on?"

During mindfulness meditation you take your attention away from all else that is going on in your life – all your usual, repetitive thoughts. Instead, you take control of your mind and use it to pay full attention to your whole body, your thoughts and your emotional feelings, or the silence and the space that can be found within.

Normally we focus on things briefly and not consciously, flitting from one thing to the next as quickly as possible in our minds. When meditating you focus on something specific, which allows your mind to slow down and become calm. By doing this you can be fully in the here and now, exploring inside yourself, so that you can observe and understand your mind and emotions, and find the peace inside of you. "Meditation offers the opportunity for each of us to create what is effectively a sacred space in which to nurture a sense of wellbeing, tap our inner resources and find lasting peace of mind" (Roland, 2000).

Your inner space is your very own to do anything you want in; nobody can enter there without your permission. It is yours to enjoy. You can use it, protect it and appreciate it. Meditation is an opportunity to do this and to find sanctuary within us; we can make friends with stillness, with nothing and nobody; and it can take away many fears about being alone or relying on unreliable people for happiness – we can learn to be more emotionally independent. According to Bolte Taylor, (2009), "The secret to hooking into any of these peaceful states [experienced in meditation] is the willingness to stop the cognitive loops of thought, worry, and any ideas that distract us from the kinesthetic and sensory experience of being in the here and now."

Through meditation we can switch from doing mode to being mode, from our chattering left hemispheres to our calm and creative right hemispheres. It gives us something to do (just "be") when there is nothing else to do.

The ultimate aim is to carry over this deeper calm awareness and experience it throughout the day so that it is more than a practice – it is a state of mind. Meditation is merely an opportunity to develop your ability to experience the benefits in a way that is not possible during our usual day-to-day busyness.

Types of

According to Eckhart Tolle (2005), meditation is all about creating "a gap in the incessant stream of thought". There are many types of meditation practice for doing this, including mindfulness, loving kindness, the mindfulness of breath, visualisation, Transcendental Meditation, or contemplation (to increase understanding of ourselves and particular situations or to contemplate the nature of reality, as the Dalai Lama recommends in *The Art of Happiness* (1999), in order to meet life's challenges with stoicism). The main ones that I have found most useful for the purposes of encouraging relaxation and creating headspace in clients are included in this chapter and the other relevant chapters. It is not within the scope of this book to go deeply into all of them, but is intended as an introduction, so that you or your client can go on to explore other meditation practices if you have benefitted from this practice and have had your interest sparked.

Benefits

Meditation helps to develop peace of mind.

The benefits of meditation are many and can be profound. Meditation quietens, slows and calms the mind; it can help you to develop attention, mindfulness, compassion, healthy breathing habits and sense of well-being (inner peace and joy – you can discover the joy of being). Meditation encourages deep relaxation and reduces stress. For clients this space provides time away from "the voice in their head" or at least for being mindful of it and distancing themselves from it.

This can lead to deep relaxation – to release all the tensions in mind and body. It will provide an opportunity to be free of their concerns temporarily; a few minutes can be restorative and help them to find inner strength, and if they practise it regularly, it can be transformative.

Through exploring and expanding the mind you have increased space in which to accommodate "problems". It is also an opportunity to gain deep insights which can never be taught, as this awareness comes from within ourselves.

Meditation is something that can only really be understood by experiencing it for yourself.
Head space = peace.

Meditation in clinical practice

In my clinical experience, you need to have already built a level of trust with the client before introducing the idea of practising meditation. Clients are typically initially wary of the idea, but with a little encouragement they are at least willing to spare a few minutes at the end of a therapy session to give it a try – probably more to appease me than because they feel it will be of benefit to them. However, in all but one case (and I have done meditation with most clients in the last few years), they open their eyes after the practice with a peaceful smile and, when asked, report that they enjoyed it and found it helpful. In many cases, in subsequent sessions it is the main thing they want to do!

In the case of the one client who did not respond so positively, on reflection I understood that it was attempted too soon. They were too caught up in very strong emotions which overpowered them and they were unable to attend to the meditation. We also hadn't discussed the implications of emotions, thoughts and stress and the importance of dealing with these (see chapter 2: "Introducing the Idea of Working on Negative Thinking, Stress and Relaxation").

How to meditate

According to David I. Rome in *Your Body Knows the Answer* (2014), meditation "is a gentle discipline of becoming familiar with the open, nonconceptual space in ourselves that is always available once we know how to find and rest in it". Here is how to set up and create a meditation session.

- First decide which meditation would be most beneficial for the client.

- Position: the client can find the position that suits them best, but in the therapy session it will likely be easier to sit on a chair as described in the chapter on posture.

- Clients can keep their eyes open, but it will be easier to focus if they are closed.

- Client listens to a meditation CD or to you in the therapy session.

- When you read a guided meditation with a client, be aware of your rate of speech, softness of voice and intonation. Take your time. Feel the peace yourself as you read in order to enhance the experience for the client.

Difficulties with meditation

It is common to find meditation difficult initially; it takes self-discipline, particularly if you are doing it alone. This is where listening to a guided meditation – particularly in a therapy session, or when attending a group – can be useful as it can help you stay focused.

If the client attempts to meditate alone, they need to be prepared for dealing with the challenges of meditation. According to Nigel Wellings in *Why Can't I Meditate?* (2015), these can include wanting a "good" session too much (so focusing on the goal rather than the process), aversion (avoidance, which is due to fears), sleepiness, being too restless, doubting the benefits and doubting our ability to engage effectively. Participants who attend his meditation groups are encouraged to "turn inwards towards the experience and include it in [the] mindfulness [practice]". In other words, to see any difficulties as not something to avoid or get through as quickly as possible but for it all to be valid and part of the experience – accept and carry on.

Summary

- Meditation involves consciously directing your attention on something, such as the breath.

- Meditation helps to calm the mind and create space within, resulting in peace.

- From this calmer state of being, clients are able to respond more effectively in therapy and in their daily lives.

- Meditation is powerful but needs to be experienced to be fully understood. Introducing the practice within a therapy session allows clients the opportunity to do this and understand the benefits, and it only need take a few minutes.

- Meditating alone can be challenging initially. Being guided in a therapy session can increase the chance of clients experiencing a "successful" meditation.

Activities

Guided meditations

There are many guided meditations throughout the book and many more that you can find in other meditation books, but here are a few more to choose from:

- See what happens in the space – awareness will create its own images to watch.

  "Make yourself comfortable. Sit back against the chair, feet on the floor. Imagine there is a string attached to the top of your head pulling your head upwards, and in turn straightening your spine. Let your shoulders hang down and rest your hands comfortably in your lap.

  "Focus on your breath. Just observe it. Let your breath come and go; there is no need to control it.

  "All your muscles are relaxing more and more. Relaxation is spreading throughout your body from your scalp and forehead, cheeks, tongue. Your eyeballs soften. Your neck, shoulders, arms, all the way past your elbows to your wrists, hands and fingers. Your chest and back, your stomach, your legs all the way down past your knees to your ankles, your feet and toes. You are becoming more and more relaxed. More and more calm. If your mind wanders just gently bring your awareness back to your body.

  "Look inside yourself and be aware of nothing but space, perhaps just like being in space surrounded by stars. Now just watch. Notice if any images come to mind, what do you see? Notice any colours. Notice how things are changing. Notice also any thoughts that come to mind. Welcome them. Perhaps comment on them – "oh, that one again." Or perhaps it's a useful idea. Then gently bring your mind back to the space and see what happens. If nothing comes to mind, enjoy the peace that is in the space, in the nothingness. Just stay ready to watch any changes, observe them and allow them to happen without trying to control.

  "Take a few moments to do this, and when you are ready become aware of the chair you are sitting on, the sounds in the room, and then in your own time open your eyes."

- Becoming transparent.

  "Make yourself comfortable. Sit back against the chair, feet on the floor. Imagine there is a string attached to the top of your head pulling your head upwards, and in turn straightening your spine. Let your shoulders hang down and rest your hands comfortably in your lap. Focus on your breath. Just observe it. Let your breath come and go; there is no need to control it. All your muscles are relaxing more and more. Relaxation is spreading throughout your body from your scalp and forehead, cheeks, tongue. Your eyeballs soften. Your neck, shoulders, arms, all the way past your elbows to your wrists hands and fingers. Your chest and back, your stomach, your legs all the way down past your knees to your ankles, your feet and toes. You are becoming more and more relaxed. More and more calm. If your mind wanders just gently bring your awareness back to your body.

"As you are aware of your body you notice it is now transparent, the air goes through you, you are space. Any issues or problems you had just go through you. You are formless, without form. Nothing has any effect on you; everything goes through you. When people direct their negative feelings at you, they too go straight through you. You have let go of the form to which things meet resistance and stick to. Everything comes and goes without you holding onto it. You are only conscious of the space right here. Anything that happens goes quickly. You are aware of what is happening here and now only, in this room. You can do this whenever you are in situations you normally find difficult or with people you find challenging.

"When you are ready, become aware of the chair you are sitting on, the sounds in the room, and then in your own time, open your eyes."

Other ways to meditate

- Walking meditation – walk around the room, or outside. Walk very slowly, focusing on your breath and how your body feels. Slowly lift up one foot and move it consciously forward, then place the heel carefully on the floor, followed by the ball of the foot, and slowly shift the whole body forward as you the begin to repeat with the other foot. Keep your eyes focused just ahead of you, be aware of what you see. Keep your mind focused as you walk. Keep reminding the client of the instructions if you are with them. Allow 5–10 minutes for this.

- Listen to Gregorian chants or similar relaxing music.

- Hum – "mmm". This can be used to help prepare for another meditation or as a meditation practice by itself. According to Sondra Barrett in *Secrets of Your Cells* (2013), who advocates practising this for several minutes every day to enhance well-being, "Many people find that repeating a sound as a single, monotonous tone induces and deepens the meditative state . . . [as] when we hear and make a repetitive sound, our brain waves slow."

Note: Do not do this when driving or engaging in any other activity that requires alertness due to the slowing down of brain waves and response times.

References

Barrett, Sondra. 2013. *Secrets of Your Cells*. Boulder, CO: Sounds True Inc.

Gauding, Madonna. 2005. *The Meditation Bible*. London: Octopus Publishing Group Limited.

HH Dalai Lama and Cutler, Howard C. 1999. *The Art of Happiness*. New York: Penguin.

Roland, Paul. 2000. *How to Meditate*. London: Hamlyn.

Rome, David I. 2014. *Your Body Knows the Answer*. Boston, MA: Shambhala Publications Inc.

Taylor, Jill Bolte. 2009. *My Stroke of Insight*. London: Hodder & Stoughton.

Tolle, Eckhart. 2005. *The Power of Now*. London: Hodder & Stoughton.

Wellings, Nigel. 2015. *Why Can't I Meditate?* London: Little, Brown Book Group.

8. Visualisation

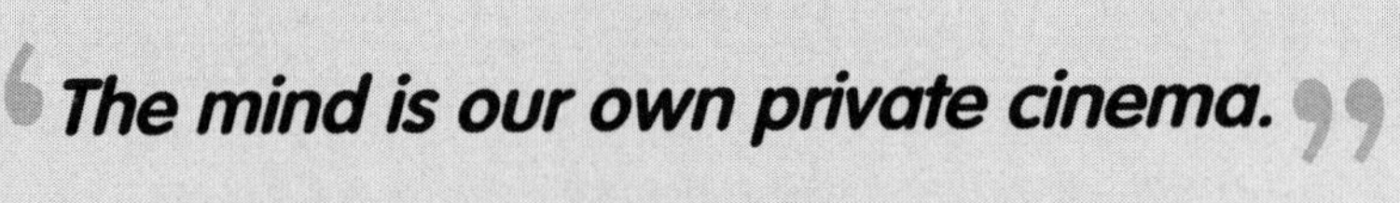

From Mike George, 1998, *Learn to Relax*.

Aims

- To learn about the possible uses and benefits of visualisation.

- To learn about obstacles to visualisation and the need to practise.

What is visualisation?

Visualisation is the conjuring up of images in our mind's eye. We frequently have images in our minds but we are not actively bringing them to mind and using them purposefully, in a controlled and constructive way.

A picture paints a thousand words.

The focus is on images, not words. Our left brain hemisphere (which is the dominant hemisphere) focuses on using "words to describe, define, categorize, and communicate about everything . . . our left mind thrives on details, details, and more details about those details" (Bolte Taylor, 2009). The circuitry in this hemisphere are not the ones you want to hook into if you want to feel relaxed and reduce tension. Visualisation harnesses the power of our right hemisphere – which thinks in pictures, giving it an opportunity to develop and by doing so quieten the overbearing left hemisphere. Neuroanatomist Jill Bolte Taylor experienced a stroke in the left hemisphere, significantly impairing her ability to use its functions; she therefore experienced first-hand the power of the right hemisphere. She goes on to say that the right hemisphere exists only in the present moment – it is in the now, which is where the experience of joy happens. Also, the right hemisphere is "spontaneous, carefree, and imaginative. It allows our artistic juices to flow free without inhibition or judgement." Without the chatter of the left hemisphere, Bolte Taylor was able to fully experience and live in the calm, joyful and creative side of her. Through practising visualisation, your client can do the same.

Creative uses for visualisation

Visualisation can be used in many ways. Here are some examples:

- To develop your sense of happiness/well-being/make yourself laugh and create joy inside yourself.

- To "clear out the cobwebs" of the mind.

- To distract yourself by taking yourself to a "happy place".

- To detach from a situation/get perspective.

- To develop resilience/inner strength/protect self.

- To improve attention.

- For goal setting/motivation. "Like a lasso thrown around a star, your imagination navigates the surest path to your goal" (John Payne, 2010).

- For physical healing (at a cellular level). (See chapter: "The Power of the Mind".)

- To mentally prepare yourself for events or situations – e.g. to practise calming your nerves for a return to work, or to visualise what you are going to do or what might happen to prepare for a sports competition. Or as the Dalai Lama encourages in *The Art of Happiness* (1999), to mentally prepare yourself for difficult times in life – such as inevitable losses. These situations will then come as less of a shock as you are more prepared for aspects of life that we try and are usually able to ignore.

- To take away fears through humour/distraction – such as the tried and trusted imagining of your audience naked or dressed in funny costumes when doing presentations.

In your mind you can jump into the space of peace and possibilities.

The mind can be your playground, or your prison. You can be free in your head – that is perhaps our true freedom.

For the purposes of this book we are focusing on using visualisation to reduce stress and tension, but I would encourage you to use your imagination when it comes to using visualisations with your client. Learning about how powerful the mind can be can give you inspiration to explore its potential. Talk it through with your client; see what they are open to and also what they can come up with for themselves.

Obstacles to creative and positive visualisation

Some clients may initially object to trying visualisation, and then on attempting, state that they can't do it. In fact they may be quite convinced about their inability to visualise "successfully".

We did have vivid imaginations, but visualisation and imagination have likely not been developed and encouraged since early childhood, and even then, only at certain times and led in certain directions. As we get older we are encouraged not to daydream but to live life in the "real world". In a world full of screens, we have also become used to mental stimulation occurring at high speed through watching and/or interacting with external things. Just as our muscles atrophy whilst we are looking at these screens, so too does our imagination. We become passive receivers of information (often sensationalised).

Mike George (1998) writes,

> Often, if the imagination works at all, it is the servant of pessimism: what would happen if I lost my job? What if my husband left me tomorrow? . . . Banishing the bleak scenario, we conjure images that enable us to see our situations . . . constructively.

Again the types of thoughts and images our minds default to are more likely to be negative if we are absorbed in unpleasant news and dramas played out on screens. But we can replace "unwanted thought patterns with vivid imagery [which] can help us shift our consciousness back toward our deep inner peace" (Bolte Taylor, 2009).

Developing the imagination to reduce stress and tension

As Roland (2000) says, "the imagination is the medium through which we *focus our mental energy* to create our own happiness or hardship in this world." As the imagination is like a muscle, it will need to "work out" to develop and become stronger. Through this practice, you will develop your ability to generate imagery in your mind and learn to control and manipulate the images to create your own "happiness" rather than your own "hardship". When actively visualising, you have the opportunity to explore your mind and see what is really there and what you can do with it.

Over time we have lost some of our powers to create in our minds, but we can reclaim them – they have just been lying dormant. The more you do it the more you are rewiring the brain, and so the more you will be in control of your mind and the more positive thoughts you will naturally have!

You can do this yourself or you can be led by a guided visualisation. This need not be an onerous task – it is something to have fun with. See the mind as an empty container you can choose how to fill. You can also choose to keep it empty, and at these times you will experience peace.

From Anita Moorjani, 2012, *Dying to Be Me*. Reprinted with permission.

Remember, you need to take more control of your mind or it will control you. Beware of letting negative thoughts and images play on a loop. For example, an elderly client who had been registered blind for many years, and was living on her own, lived in fear of having to leave her home to go into a residential home, and she would imagine herself there. This thought dominated her mind. But, whilst thinking about it she may as well have been there! Your thoughts create your world. You can create a nicer world and you can make your mind a happier place. It starts with actively engaging the mind and utilising its potential.

It is through our imaginations that we can free ourselves from anxiety and stress. Stretch your muscle – develop flexibility of thought – think differently.

You can go anywhere you want in your mind – it's free and it's freeing!

Summary

- Visualisation is the creating of mental images.

- Visualisation is taking conscious control of your thoughts to help serve you and achieve what you want.

- Using visualisations can be fun and enjoyable.

- Visualisation can be used for many purposes, including developing inner calm, creating a positive mind-set and increasing motivation.

- Visualisation needs to be practised in order to develop your ability to harness its potential.

Activities

Developing visualisation

- As your client may not feel confident in trying any kind of visualisation exercise, you may need to motivate and give them encouragement to begin with. Inform them of the differences between the dominant left and less assertive right brain hemispheres. Then try the following visualisation practices to develop their ability, confidence and faith in the benefits of visualisation.

- Ask your client to visualise a container in their mind, such as an empty bucket. Fill it with objects, one at a time. Use ordinary, everyday objects which are not detailed, such as an apple, a spoon or a green ball. Have the client look at each one in turn and manipulate the image. Can they change details – make it bigger or smaller, change the colour (perhaps to a colour they are not likely to see that object in, such as a blue apple), or add patterns such as spots or zigzags? Add more if they are able. Try making the container bigger to accommodate more. Take this exercise slowly to develop ability and confidence.

Now ask the client to empty the container – enjoy the space, and the peace.

- Another exercise to develop visualisation – ask your client to visualise walking around their house. Or even just one room. Look around carefully, noticing all the objects, colours and details they can recall.

Scenes

Beach scene

"Make yourself comfortable. Close your eyes. Sit back against the chair, feet on the floor. Imagine there is a string attached to the top of your head pulling your head upwards, and in turn straightening your spine. Let your shoulders hang down and rest your hands comfortably in your lap.

"Focus on your breath. Just observe it. Let your breath come and go; there is no need to control it.

"All your muscles are relaxing more and more. Relaxation is spreading throughout your body from your scalp and forehead, cheeks, tongue. Your eyeballs soften. Your neck, shoulders, arms, all the way past your elbows to your wrists hands and fingers. Your chest and back, your stomach, your legs all the way down past your knees to your ankles, your feet and toes. You are becoming more and more relaxed. More and more calm. If your mind wanders just gently bring your awareness back to your body.

"Now imagine yourself on a sandy beach. There is no one else around. The sun is shining overhead; you close your eyes and enjoy feeling the warmth from the sun. You listen to the sound of the waves gently lapping against the pebbly shore. The sand beneath your feet is soft and warm. You feel the gentlest of breezes on your skin; it is warm and comforting. As you stand there on the beach you find you are becoming more and more relaxed, more and more calm.

"After a few moments you begin to slowly walk along the beach. As you take one slow step at a time, feel the sand beneath your feet. Feel the breeze. Feel and enjoy the space, you have this beach all to yourself, no one can see you. You are free here.

"You find a spot to sit down and watch the waves. You notice seagulls in the distance and can hear their muffled calls. Their familiar sounds only make you feel more and more relaxed. You now focus on the waves. You watch them gently coming in, and going out. Gently coming in, and out. You notice that the tide is very slowly receding away from you. Take a few moments to enjoy watching the motion of the waves.

"Now you feel like you would like to lie back on the sand. Your eyes are closed. You are enjoying feeling the warm, soft sand beneath you and the warm rays of the sun above. As you lie there enjoying the warmth and hearing the sound of the waves you feel more and more calm, more and more relaxed, more and more serene. Take a few moments to enjoy this blissful setting.

"Now, when you are ready, start to be aware of the chair you are sitting on. Be aware of any sounds in this room. Feel your feet on the floor. When you are ready, slowly open your eyes."

Woodland walk

Begin meditation as above.

"You find yourself in a clearing in the middle of a wood. You are all alone, but you know you are perfectly safe. In the clearing you notice all kinds of flowers in the long grass. All around are a variety of trees giving off wonderful smells. In-between the trees are an abundance of bluebells. Above you the sky is blue, and the sun is shining. It is a very warm day.

"You notice a path and you begin to walk through the woods. You are aware of the sounds of birds around you. Breathe deeply and smell the trees and the flowers. Enjoy the cooler, fresher air of the woods. You look up to see some sunlight coming through the canopy of the woods. You notice how green the leaves are with the sun shining through them. As you go deeper into the wood you feel calmer, and calmer. You are in a safe haven.

"You come to the edge of the woods, where you find a stream. You sit on the grassy bank with your legs dangling down so that your feet and ankles are submerged in the water. You lie back, keeping your feet in the stream. You have your eyes closed. Listen to the stream. Feel the water flow gently around your feet. It is pleasantly cool after your walk. Feel the long grass beneath you; you are very comfortable and very relaxed. Listen to the birds . . . feel the warmth of the sun . . . smell the flowers. Feel how heavy your body is; it is fully supported. You become more and more calm, more and more serene. Enjoy this blissful place for a few moments.

"When you are ready, slowly get up from beside the stream. Start to walk slowly back through the woods, where you find the clearing. When you are ready, start to be aware of the chair you are sitting on. Be aware of any sounds in this room. Feel your feet on the floor. When you are ready, slowly open your eyes."

Return to work

This is a sample meditation that was successfully used with a client, and includes affirmations (see chapter: "Affirmations"). You will want to adapt this to suit the circumstances of your client.

"As we go through the following visualisation we are going to use some affirmations. Affirmations are things we tell ourselves repeatedly to encourage particular thoughts and feelings.

"You can choose how you feel. The more you tell yourself how you want to feel the more you will feel it. But you need to say it with joyful enthusiasm, even if you don't believe it too much to begin with. All you have to do is keep telling yourself positive things and you will start to believe it more and more. The more you focus on positive thoughts and feelings the less opportunity you have to sabotage your efforts with negativity. The more positive you are the more successful you will be.

"You can choose how you think and feel, and you can choose to be happy and positive. You have to work at being happy and positive about things. You can get into the habit of being happy and positive. You can replace negative self-talk with positive affirmations.

"Repetition, repetition, repetition and gusto are key to powerful affirmations and a positive mental attitude.

"Visualisation and humour together with affirmations are powerful ways to make you more positive and happy, and more ready to face any challenges.

"You can control what goes on in your head.

"It is the morning of your return to work. You are standing outside the building where you work. However, imagine there are two of you. The two of you look at each other; one of you says to the other:

"I am SO pleased to be going back to work."

The other one replies:

"Yes, so am I!"

The first one repeats several times: "I am SO pleased to be going back to work." Repeat this three times.

The first one then says: "I have faith; I do not need to worry as everything is as is it should be."

The two of you look so happy. You give each other a hug. You know you can rely on each other for support.

You both walk in. You see your colleagues. As you greet them, you repeat loudly in your head:

"I am SO pleased to be back here. I feel happy and calm." Repeat this three times.

You go in to your manager's office. As they are discussing things with you, you are aware that you are smiling and nodding.

You repeat loudly in your head:

"I am SO pleased to be back here. I feel happy and calm. I am ready to get on with work."

You walk over to your computer with your manager. As they help you log on you realise this feels so familiar. You have done this many times before.

You repeat loudly in your head: "I am so pleased to be back here. I feel happy and calm. I am ready to get on with work. I am not worried about having any difficulties. I have supportive colleagues. I can ask for help if I need it. And that is fine. My colleagues will expect that. I am so happy to be back at work."

You sit alone at your computer and start your work. Imagine yourself doing a typical task. The other you sits next to you and you look at the work together. You are a team. You remind each other not to worry if you're not sure about something. You are there to support each other. You repeat loudly to yourself: "I am happy to be back at my desk getting on with my work. I welcome any challenges. I welcome the opportunity to work my brain and make it stronger. I know that my brain works better the more I use it and test it. I know that that my brain continues to learn and get stronger all the time. I learn and move on, and then I learn new things."

After you finish this task, you say goodbye to your colleagues and leave. Outside your two selves hug and thank each other for the others' support. You know you both want the best for you.

You repeat loudly to yourself: "I feel positive about my return to work. I am glad I have completed my first day, and I am looking forward to coming back again. I am happy I have taken this step. I am moving on."

In a few moments I will count from one to three. When I reach the count of three, your eyes will open and you will feel completely refreshed and totally relaxed.

1. . . 2. . . 3

Repeat as necessary.

Other visualisation techniques to aid relaxation

- Encourage your client to see what comes to them – thoughts/images/colours.

- Visualise music passing through the head – clearing out the cobwebs.

- Visualise an orchestra whilst listening to classical music – imagine conducting it. Tune in to each instrument you hear.

- Ask your client to visualise themselves there in the room. Then imagine the building – look down on it. Now see the whole street, zoom out to see the town, then the county, the whole country, the continent, the whole of planet Earth as if you are in space. Zoom out further to see more and more of the solar system, and the Universe. Then go back in reverse order, until they are back in the room again. Getting this kind of perspective can help clients see their situation differently. Their mind expands and can accommodate more than they thought. There is a more complete meditation for this (the pure awareness technique) in Frank Kinslow's book *The Secret of Instant Healing* (2008).

Visualise black

Visualising black can be deeply relaxing and is also beneficial for vision. It involves an exercise called "palming" which according to Meir Schneider in his book *Vision for Life* (2012) helps to quiet the mind and relax the eyes. To learn more about this technique, it is worth reading his book.

With warm hands, very gently place your palms over your closed eyes, so that there is no pressure at all – the palms in fact do not touch the eyelids. Whilst in this position notice what you can see, what colours you can see. It is very unlikely you will see pure black due to the activity of the brain. But pure black is what you want to now see in your mind's eye. Schneider recommends visualising yourself and everything around you being painted black. Everything gradually becomes black, and that is all you are aware of – black. Another visualisation for palming as recommended by William Bates, in his book *Better Eyesight without Glasses* (1994), is visualising a white piece of chalk with a black spot on it. Make the black spot bigger and bigger, and blacker and blacker, until that is all you see. Avoid doing this if very stressed or angry.

- In Lesley Lyle's book *Laugh Your Way to Happiness* (2014), she recommends thinking of a person or situation that makes you smile. Take time to enjoy this

Figure 8.1 Transcending the body

memory. Notice how it feels, be aware of the energy you feel inside when recalling this memory. As you breathe in allow this feeling to go with your breath to your lungs, and then around your whole body. Do this for several breaths. "Slowly open your eyes, with a smile on your face!"

Letting go of the physical confines of the body and giving up the struggle

- Encourage your client to visualise a clear mind and a clear body. Inside themselves is empty – no thoughts (to create tension), no muscles (to feel tension). They can do this for a few moments, and throughout the day to help themselves get a sense of freedom from physical and emotional baggage.

- Visualise transcending the body – you can leave it in your mind – there is no need to be within its confines. Let go. Step out of your body. You are separate from it. You are formless. You are invisible. Your client can be led straight into another meditation where they are not in the confines of the body – flying, floating, as described here below.

- Claire Weekes in her book *Self-Help for Your Nerves* (1995) encourages clients who are terrified of a situation to imagine floating there, instead of forcing themselves through. She also encourages allowing the thoughts themselves to float away (out of the head) or to "float . . . past obstructive thoughts" in order to overcome paralysing tension, as the paralysis "lies in the thoughts not the muscles."

Enjoying the freedom of space

Begin meditation as described above for the scenes.

"Now imagine yourself in space, surrounded by nothing but distant stars. Breathing is no problem in this space, nor is moving. You are quite happy floating through space with no restrictions. You can move freely. You can move slowly or fast if you prefer, or change speeds. It is up to you.

"You are now aware of a trapeze in front of you. You instinctively grab hold of it and take a big swing as if it were attached to really long ropes. You let go, but you know there is no need to worry, as immediately another one appears that you can easily grab hold of. Again you take a big swing and have no fears, because as soon as you let go another one appears. Take a few moments to enjoy moving freely through space. Enjoy the space – which goes on forever; enjoy the silence, the peace, the freedom.

"When you are ready, start to be aware of the chair you are sitting on. Be aware of any sounds in this room. Feel your feet on the floor. When you are ready, slowly open your eyes."

Swimming in the lake

Begin meditation as described above for the scenes.

"Imagine standing by the side of a lake. It is in a beautiful countryside surrounded by meadows and hills. The sun is shining; you are enjoying its warmth. It is very warm here. There is no one else around; you are all alone.

"You walk over to a small jetty. You are already in your swimming costume, and you start to feel the temperature get hotter and hotter. The lake looks so inviting. You dive into the cool, refreshing water. You find that you are not restricted in your movements in the water, in fact you can move swiftly and easily like a dolphin. You can dive down into the lake as deep as you want and for as long as you want – breathing is not an issue here. You swim with speed under the water, then up towards the surface, break through the surface, up into the air, then dive gracefully back into the water. You enjoy taking the time to explore what you are capable of in this water, and enjoy the freedom of movement. There is no resistance in the water, you move with ease and joy.

"After a while, you enjoy floating on the surface of the water, again this is easy to do, there is no effort involved. Enjoy the calm, the peace, the tranquillity of the setting you find yourself in.

"When you are ready you swim over to the jetty, where you find a ladder. You climb out, and lie on a hammock that you notice nearby. Enjoy relaxing here; the weight of your body is fully supported. You become more and more calm, more and more serene.

"When you are ready, start to be aware of the chair you are sitting on. Be aware of any sounds in this room. Feel your feet on the floor. When you are ready, slowly open your eyes."

Colour visualisations

- According to Vijaya Kumar in her book *Colour Therapy* (2003), "Colour influences our energy system by its vibrations, affecting both our physical and emotional well-being. . . . Each colour radiates its own particular vibration to which we respond." Therefore, colours can be incorporated into visualisations for deep relaxation. You will find another useful colour visualisation in June McLeod's book *Colours of the Soul* (2006).

A simple colour visualisation is to sit with eyes closed, gradually relax and see what colours come into your mind's eye. You may see particular colours that are beneficial and therapeutic to you. Allow a few minutes to relax and focus on these colours. Watch what they do and how they change.

Self-Protection

- Visualisation can be used to help protect yourself from difficult people and situations. You and your inner space need to be more guarded at certain times, and there are various ways to feel more protected on the inside through visualisation. You can imagine yourself in a bubble; Vijaya Kumar (2003) recommends that this bubble should be white, as this is a protective energy. You can float in this bubble, and you can make it your "happy bubble" where no outside forces can disturb you. The more vivid the visualisation the more effectively it will work. Using humour also helps!

References

Bates, William H. 1994. *Better Eyesight without Glasses*. London: Thorsons.

George, Mike. 1998. *Learn to Relax*. London: Duncan Baird Publishers.

HH Dalai Lama and Cutler, Howard C. 1999. *The Art of Happiness*. New York: Penguin.

John Payne, Kim. 2010. *Simplicity Parenting*. New York, NY: Ballantine Books.

Kinslow, Frank J. 2008. *The Secret of Instant Healing*. London: Hay House UK Ltd.

Kumar, Vijaya. 2003. *Colour Therapy*. New Delhi: New Dawn Press Inc.

Lyle, Lesley. 2014. *Laugh Your Way to Happiness*. Oxford: Watkins Publishing Limited.

McLeod, June. 2006. *Colours of the Soul*. Ropley, Hants: O Books.

Moorjani, Anita. 2012. *Dying to Be Me*. Carlsbad, CA: Hay House Inc.

Roland, Paul. 2000. *How to Meditate*. London: Hamlyn.

Schneider, Meir. 2012. *Vision for Life: Ten Steps to Natural Eyesight Improvement*. Berkeley, CA: North Atlantic Books.

Taylor, Jill Bolte. 2009. *My Stroke of Insight*. London: Hodder & Stoughton.

Weekes, Claire. 1995. *Self-Help for Your Nerves*. London: Thorsons.

9. The power of the mind

Know your power.

Aims

- To help therapists and clients to believe in the power of the mind, so that they can begin to trust in it more and start to utilise it.

- To help clients harness the power of their minds in the way that they want in order to help themselves.

- To increase self-confidence.

- To understand the power of a client's mind in undermining efforts to improve in therapy.

- To encourage therapists and clients to start thinking creatively about how they can use this amazing power to optimise their therapy sessions/life.

We are more powerful than we think! We are not so helpless

There is now a growing body of research which is demonstrating the enormous potential each of us has within in us – "What you think and feel, how you talk to yourself, and what view you take about what is happening to you and around you has a powerful impact on your health and well-being" (Brantley, 2003). According to scientist David Hamilton (2008) who worked for several years in the pharmaceutical industry studying the effects of the placebo, "We are barely scratching the surface in our understanding of real human potential."

When it comes to health, this emerging evidence shows that there is less and less reason to adopt the "sick role", to feel helpless and believe "this is it" – these are the circumstances I have been given, this is my fate, this is what my genes have determined. We are programmed to give our power away when it comes to the healing of our bodies, and to begin to consider that you don't always need to do this, and to believe we have the power within us takes faith, and understandably, for most people, evidence – which is now coming through.

The mind and our consciousness are also proving to affect life and experiences beyond ourselves. This is a huge area for you to explore if you are interested, which is for the most part not within the scope of this book. This chapter is merely an introduction, to make you aware of this increasing understanding and acceptance in scientific communities. However, the more you grow in awareness and understanding of the power of the mind, the more faith you will have in your own mind and also that of your client's to have profound effects on themselves, and so affect the course of therapy.

We are made of energy

> **Ultimately the mind [is] the instrument that create[s] our picture of reality. The mind cause[s] us to see matter where really only vibrations of energy exist.**
>
> David R. Hamilton

From David R. Hamilton, 2008, *How Your Mind Can Heal Your Body*. Reprinted with permission.

Although we take it for granted that we are solid, we are actually just waves of energy. The fact that we appear solid is an illusion due to how our brains have been wired to perceive our external reality. According to David Hamilton in *How Your Mind Can Heal Your Body* (2008), when you get down to the subatomic level of cells (our building blocks) where you find the protons, electrons and neutrons (which are actually vibrations of energy and can change easily, Tolle (2005) describes them as "like a musical note"), there is mostly empty space (this space is known as the *quantum field*), which in fact resembles the night sky. The distance between the stars and planets correspond proportionally to the distances between the waves of energy in our cells. It turns out we are 99.9999999999999% space! Therefore we are made of space and energy; it is strange that we are "solid."

Our thoughts affect our bodies

> **Every cell within your body responds to every single thought you think and every word you speak.**
>
> Louise L. Hay

From Louise Hay, 1984, *You Can Heal Your Life*. Reprinted with permission.

Thoughts have the power to affect the "physical matter" of our bodies. Thoughts are again vibrations of energy, so when you understand that our supposedly solid bodies are likewise energy, it is easier to make the leap and see that the energy of the mind can affect the body, as the energy vibrations change the vibrations of other molecules around them – think of waves in water and how they can change and how they transfer their energy throughout the body of water.

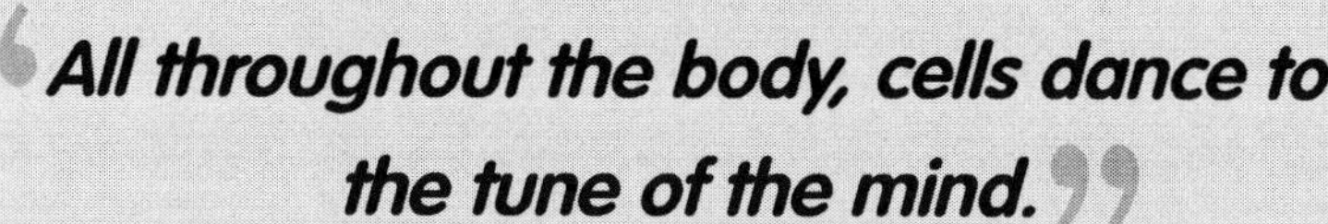

David R. Hamilton

From David R. Hamilton, 2008, *How Your Mind Can Heal Your Body*. Reprinted with permission.

Thought energy can thus resonate throughout our whole bodies and change our physiology. They work at the level of the cellular membrane; there they activate proteins that in turn affect DNA. In fact, Bruce Lipton, a renowned cell biologist, writes in his book *The Biology of Belief* (2015), "It is not our gene-directed hormones and neurotransmitters that control our bodies and our minds: our beliefs control our bodies and our minds, and thus our lives." To realise that genetic determinism is a myth is hugely empowering – we have the ability to change the course of our lives by changing our thoughts, beliefs and of course our subsequent lifestyle choices – this is known as the science of epigenetics ("control above genetics"). "DNA does not control our biology; instead, DNA is controlled by signals from outside the cell, including the energetic messages emanating from our positive and negative thoughts" (Lipton, 2015). As Gill Edwards, a clinical psychologist, writes in *Conscious Medicine* (2010), "it is our consciousness that controls our biology." Our consciousness is "The CEO of our body" – we can switch genes on and off; we are not inevitabilities.

Our thoughts and beliefs can help and heal us, or hurt us

Once you understand that your mind can control your body, you are able to reflect on the types of thoughts you have and the messages they are sending to your body – are they positive or negative? Helpful or harmful? "You can be a healthier person by recognising and managing the power of your own thoughts and emotions!" (Brantley, 2003).

> ❝ **The belief that we are frail, biochemical machines controlled by genes is giving way to an understanding that we are powerful creators of our lives and the world in which we live.** ❞
>
> Bruce H. Lipton

From Bruce H. Lipton, 2015, *The Biology of Belief 10th Anniversary Edition.* Reprinted with permission. (Emphasis in original.)

Feeling good psychologically and having an overall sense of optimism helps us physically in every way. According to Irving Kirsch, a clinical psychologist, in his book *The Emperor's New Drugs* (2009), it makes us feel good physically, helps maintain a healthy blood pressure, improves immune function, aids recovery from heart surgery, and even cancer survival may be affected by emotional well-being. It is also possible to use the power of our minds to "override autonomic controls such as body temperature, blood pressure, and pH" (Lipton, 2015) and control our heart rate and reduce our breathing.

Effects of perceptions and interpretations

> ❝ *Optimism protects you from illness.* ❞
>
> *David R. Hamilton*

From David R. Hamilton, 2008, *How Your Mind Can Heal Your Body.* Reprinted with permission.

Optimists – people who are hopeful and see the good in situations, have repeatedly been shown to have better health outcomes than pessimists. It comes down to our perceptions and interpretations of our circumstances. Viktor Frankl, in *Man's Search for Meaning* (2004), describes his experiences in Nazi concentration camps and reflects on what determined a person's chances of survival. He concluded that it wasn't youth or physical strength which determined whether you survived, as younger, physically stronger people could succumb sooner than the older and physically weaker ones; it was finding meaning in the situation they found themselves in – this was a source of strength for mind and body, the source of this was in the mind.

Managing panic and fear

Fear arises because of our interpretation of a situation based on what information our senses have picked up from our bodies and surrounding environment. But according to Jeff Brantley, we can use our higher centres of our brains to consciously generate thoughts to "override the fear system and turn it down."

Ageing

Our thinking has also been shown to affect the ageing process. Deepak Chopra (1993) writes "[Your] biological age responds to [your] psychological age", and he encourages us to nurture our "inner life . . . to defeat aging at its source . . . [whereas] on the other hand . . . apathy, helplessness, and dissatisfaction push the body into rapid decline."

The nun study

Aging and Alzheimer's Disease: Lessons from the Nun Study (Snowden, 1997) was a study of more than 600 nuns in America that demonstrated how powerful attitudes were on the manifestation of Alzheimer's disease (or lack of). These nuns were monitored for cognitive ability and then had their brains examined when they died. The results clearly showed that how the nuns lived their life (they remained very active) prevented the expected cognitive decline even when they had significant signs of Alzheimer's disease in their brain. The nun who was primarily written about in the study and described as the "gold standard" was remembered as being "there in the present moment with all her heart and soul." According to the author "the nuns study may provide unique clues about the etiology of aging and Alzheimer's disease, exemplify what is possible in old age, and show how the clinical expression of some diseases may be averted."

Visualisation

Visualisation, in addition to aiding relaxation (see chapter: "Visualisation") has also been proven to heal or improve conditions. David Hamilton (2008) describes many studies that have proven visualisation to be effective with many conditions, including Parkinson's disease, asthma, chronic fatigue syndrome (also known as myalgic encephalomyelitis) and stroke.

Affirmations

Affirmations (see also chapter: "Affirmations") are also a useful tool to consciously control the body, improve your sense of well-being and they can positively alter a client's approach to therapy. They can also be used in conjunction with visualisations – for example, to ward off colds and flu or relieve yourself of a headache, or to help warm you up – "My immune system is amazing at fighting off flu!", or "I am super healthy!", or "I am feeling really warm!" Remember repetition is the key and saying them with feeling.

It really is a case of mind over matter.

Thoughts give rise to emotions, and positive thoughts and emotions transfer positive mental energy to positive physical energy. "When we feel positive emotions such as unconditional love, joy, passion, hope and appreciation, our bodymind soaks in healthy biochemistry" (Edwards, 2010).

Thoughts can hurt us

> **"*A negative thought can kill you faster than a bad germ. One of the main things to detoxify is here [pointing to head]. . . . The mind.*"**
>
> Antonio Jimenez

From Antonio Jimenez, 2015, in *The Truth about Cancer: A Global Quest, Transcripts*. Reprinted with permission.

There are many examples of how our thoughts have the power to physically hurt us. Any negative thoughts and emotions such as anger, resentment, shame, frustration or guilt can impact on immune function, particularly if they are carried around with us for long periods – they are emotional baggage. Anger and hostility are particularly significant risk factors for heart disease, and of course stressful thinking affects how our whole body functions, for example our ability to heal wounds, or rather to allow our body to heal itself, as these negative energies are in fact barriers to allowing the body to function in the healthy way it is supposed to.

> **"*The research is very clear; toxic thoughts are as damaging to your body as external toxins. They set in motion a self-destructive stress response.*"**
>
> Patricia Worby

From Patricia Worby, 2015, *The Scar That Won't Heal*. Reprinted with permission.

Memories

Thought and emotional responses occur both in response to situations we are currently in but also remembered or anticipated situations (imaginary). Your mind and body will process and experience it in the same way. Therefore you will want to be conscious of your thinking, such as any negative memories you replay on a loop, as these will have the same negative physiological implications as if you were still physically in the situation.

Placebos and nocebos

Placebos are another demonstration of how powerful the mind is, they "are part of a broader phenomenon – the power of suggestion to change how people feel, how they behave, and even their physiology" (Kirsch, 2009). David R. Hamilton (2008) writes how placebos are thought of as a "nuisance" in clinical pharmacological research, but are now evolving to being thought of as "a biological phenomenon worthy of scientific investigation in [their] own right."

> **Studies have shown that, for some conditions, regardless of whether a surgery is real or not, if you believe that it is (and why wouldn't you) and are optimistic about it you will receive the same benefits as if you have actually had surgery.**
>
> David R. Hamilton

From David R. Hamilton, 2008, *How Your Mind Can Heal Your Body*. Reprinted with permission.

It has been demonstrated that drugs work more effectively if we believe they will work, because they give hope (which actually comes from within us). Beliefs can affect to what extent medication works, for example because of how convincing the doctor is when telling us about the benefits, or even because of how the pill looks or smells; medications may only be slightly better than placebos. Surgery is the most powerful placebo due to higher expectations of patients that bigger changes will occur. For example, "Approximately 45 per cent of patients with Parkinson's disease get better when treated with sham surgery, but only 14 per cent of Parkinson's disease patients improve when treated with pills" (Kirsch, 2009). Kirsch goes on to write about placebo surgery that has been used in research for the treatment of osteoarthritis of the knee, which proved to have significant benefits for up to two years. "Not only was this placebo operation effective, but it was significantly more effective than actual surgery." Clearly some operations are effective – as in emergency situations, but for chronic conditions our thoughts and beliefs are important.

> **When the . . . mind is engaged in negative suggestions that can damage health the negative effects are referred to as the nocebo effect.**
>
> Bruce H. Lipton

From Bruce H. Lipton, 2015, *The Biology of Belief 10th Anniversary Edition*. Reprinted with permission.

There are many reports of the incredible power of suggestion and belief causing detrimental effects on a patient. Patients who are told they are getting chemotherapy when they are actually getting a sugar pill may experience nausea and even hair loss. It also demonstrates that we need to be very careful what we say to clients. This is particularly important for doctors, though, as quite literally, "The power of life and death is in the tongue" (Contreras, 2015).

Beliefs, stress and the subconscious mind

Stress is a major risk factor in disease. According to Gill Edwards in her book *Conscious Medicine*, (2010) "your emotional and physical health rest not upon your genetic inheritance, but on whether you are habitually in the stress response or the relaxation response." Stress and fears originate from our beliefs – our perceptions and interpretations of situations and life in general; these are formed from the experiences we had in early childhood. Beliefs are often negative and may include feeling that you are "small, [and] insignificant . . . [or that] there is never enough time – or it drags" (Edwards, 2010). You feel afraid because you have learnt life is unpredictable and scary, and you are ultimately alone and disconnected, and then there is the fear of what will come after this life, which we have to again face alone.

Beliefs that stem from the subconscious mind are powerful because the subconscious mind is "more than a million times more powerful that the conscious mind" and "shape[s] 95 per cent or more or our life experiences" (Lipton, 2015). Our subconscious is an emotional database which stores information we learnt about the world before the age of seven. When we try to overcome deep-seated (in the subconscious mind) fears with our conscious mind, it is clear it won't work if you consciously tell yourself what you want to believe just once or twice. You need to reprogram the subconscious mind by repeating, repeating, repeating affirmations. Other ways to reprogram the subconscious include Emotional Freedom Technique (EFT), hypnotherapy or Eye Movement Desensitisation and Reprocessing (EMDR). By doing this you will experience a more profound change within rather than trying to reason with your subconscious, which simply does not have the ability to respond to reason.

Our thoughts can affect other things and people and in other times

Briefly entering the realm of quantum physics here, our minds have been shown to have an effect on things outside ourselves. In *It's the Thought That Counts*, David Hamilton (2005) describes how Japanese scientist Masaru Emoto wrote down positive words such as "love", "thank you", and "Mother Teresa", and he also wrote some negative words, and put each one on to bottles of water. He then photographed them after they turned to ice. The positive words produced highly crystalline sparkly ice crystals, but negative words produced dull and undefined ice crystals. Hamilton writes, "everything is connected at a quantum level, and so my awareness of the water immediately changed it – the word I was aware of, as I thought of the water, changed it." Hamilton also had similar results when repeating the experiment with cress seeds.

This quantum level or *quantum field* is also known as the matrix, the collective consciousness and the infinite intelligence. According to quantum physics, at this level we and every cell are joined together, like a spider's web – touching one part of the web will affect the rest of it, or a particular part of it. Jill Bolte Taylor, the *New York Times* best-selling author of *My Stroke of Insight* (2009) and renowned neuroanatomist describes it in this way –

> everything around us, about us, among us and within us is made up of energy particles that are woven together into a universal tapestry. Since everything is connected, there is an intimate relationship between the atomic space around and within me, and the atomic space around and within you – regardless of where we are.

This is how distant healing works, and according to quantum physics can take place across time, as the quantum field is outside of time.

There are many other studies proving the power of the mind, such as how people have managed to twist and untwist DNA in test tubes in a distant laboratory just with their minds, and partners having an effect on each other when a strong reaction is provoked in them – as witnessed on MRI scans – even though they were in separate rooms at either end of the corridor.

Understanding how everything is connected, we can use this in positive ways such as sending healing energy to wounds ("On an energetic level . . . sending . . . energy to you with a healing intention," Edwards, 2010) or literally "sending our love" – this thought energy will reach the person or persons you send it to, and that positive energy will naturally benefit you, but of course you can always send it directly to yourself. Hamilton (2008) tells of how he "pings" love to people in creative ways, and sometimes even gets a response – people looking sad will look up at him with a smile.

Neuroplasticity

Research over recent decades shows that the brain is not fixed after childhood; it actually has an amazing ability to change and to learn by forming new neurons and new connections between neurons. This is known as "neuroplasticity". We are able to develop and rewire our brains even after brain trauma. As much as our brains may feel full, that they have reached capacity, this is absolutely not true. With some self-discipline we can work our brains and learn new skills and languages, or develop flexibility of thought and, as the Dalai Lama (1999) advocates, cultivate compassion and other positive mental states. It is too easy to stick with what we know, which hinders new connections being formed in the brain. Norman Doidge (2008) acknowledges, "Freud was right when he said that the absence of plasticity seemed related to force of habit".

Believe in the mind.

Mindfulness and the power of the mind

By mindfully observing your thoughts, beliefs and emotions you can explore your mind and create space between "you" (the observer) and your thoughts (this separation gives you more control over them and them less control over you), and then make more conscious choices with the understanding that fuelling negative thoughts and beliefs are harmful to you and those around you (remember your energy is felt on the quantum level).

When you are observing mindfully without judgement, this takes away the fear of your thoughts. There is simply no need to judge a thought as being unacceptable – you can allow it to be and let it go in its own time. As you are less distracted by these thoughts and the fear they create you can concentrate on using your mind to its full potential.

The power of the mind and therapy

Understanding the power of the mind and beliefs, it is now clear that a client's belief in you and the therapy you are trying to do will significantly impact on the therapy process and actual outcomes, as will the belief that they have in themselves and the beliefs that they have about their condition/issues and expectations about possible outcomes. Bearing this in mind you need to consider how you are coming across to the client (see chapter: "Self-Observation and Self-Awareness: Bedside Manner") to inspire belief, and also to discuss their expectations of themselves and the therapy process. Explore beliefs to see if any are unhelpful and need correcting.

Note: It is unlikely to be appropriate to talk about the power of the mind in relation to physical healing, but you can talk about placebos, nocebos and neuroplasticity. You can also advise that there are books available for your client to explore the power of the mind further for themselves, and make their own choices about how they could utilise this.

"If you believe you can or you believe you can't . . . you're right."

– attributed to Henry Ford

Summary

- Our minds are amazing, and there is a growing awareness of their potential.

- Understanding this power, you and your client can utilise it for their benefit in therapy, including to increase self-confidence.

Activities

- Discuss the power of the mind to an appropriate depth – not all clients will be open to discussing quantum physics and sending themselves love, but you can discuss neuroplasticity to increase their faith in their minds and how thoughts affect their body – positively and negatively.

- Use affirmations with the client to increase faith in their ability, or at least their ability to try, in therapy tasks.

- Encourage the client to reflect at the end of every day all that they have to be grateful for. They can enjoy the positive feelings and know they are also helping their "physical" body.

References

Brantley, Jeffrey. 2003. *Calming Your Anxious Mind*. Oakland, CA: New Harbinger Publications.

Chopra, Deepak. 1993. *Ageless Body, Timeless Mind*. New York, NY: Harmony Books.

Contreras, Francisco. 2015. In *The Truth about Cancer: A Global Quest, Transcripts*, p. 159.

Doidge, Norman. 2008. *The Brain That Changes Itself*. London: Penguin Books.

Edwards, Gill. 2010. *Conscious Medicine*. London: Little, Brown Book Group.

Frankl, Viktor. 2004. *Man's Search for Meaning*. London: Rider & Co.

Hamilton, David R. PhD. 2005. *It's the Thought That Counts*. London: Hay House UK Ltd.

Hamilton, David R. PhD. 2008. *How Your Mind Can Heal Your Body*. London: Hay House UK Ltd.

Hay, Louise L. 1984. *You Can Heal Your Life*. Carlsbad, CA: Hay House Inc.

HH Dalai Lama and Cutler, Howard C. 1999. *The Art of Happiness*. New York: Penguin.

Jimenez, Antonio. 2015. In *The Truth about Cancer: A Global Quest, Transcripts*, p. 160.

Kirsch, Irving. 2009. *The Emperor's New Drugs*. London: Bodley Head.

Lipton, Bruce H. PhD. 2015. *The Biology of Belief 10th Anniversary Edition*. London: Hay House Inc.

Snowden, David A. PhD. 1997. Aging and Alzheimer's Disease: Lessons from the Nun Study. *The Gerontologist, 37* (2), 150–156.

Taylor, Jill Bolte. 2009. *My Stroke of Insight*. London: Hodder & Stoughton.

Tolle, Eckhart. 2005. *The Power of Now*. London: Hodder & Stoughton.

Worby, Patricia. 2015. *The Scar That Won't Heal*. CreateSpace Independent Publishing Forum.

10. Affirmations

From Louise Hay, 2004, *I Can Do It*. Reprinted with permission.

Aims

- To understand the power of thoughts and beliefs – affirmations (spoken and unspoken).

- To learn the benefits of encouraging clients to become aware of their own affirmations and consciously creating their affirmations to help them achieve what they want in therapy.

What are affirmations?

Affirmations are anything you say or think – they are your thoughts and your beliefs. As you start to become aware of your thoughts and beliefs you will realise they are not always (or even very often) pleasant. In fact, they are usually very negative, for example, "I can't do it," "I'm no good at drawing," "I can't sing," "This is all awful," "I hate winter," "I have got so much to do," "This is so miserable." Think of the force behind each of these sort of thoughts, the noises we make with them – we usually really feel it! This is our interpretation and our experience of life if we are not conscious. You can use mindfulness to naturally dissipate them, but you can also challenge what you are thinking then take responsibility and choose to think differently. The difficulty we have is that we learnt these thoughts and beliefs from a young age and we have repeated them to ourselves, mostly unconsciously ever since, therefore they are hard-wired into our brains.

We create our lives and ourselves with our thoughts and beliefs, which become self-fulfilling prophecies or ". . . 'cycles of self-reinforcement.' This means that we tend to influence events in a way that's in accordance with our beliefs" (Houel with Godefroy, 1994). This often happens in a negative way. For example, if you are a "technophobe" and you are given a high-tech gadget for a present, you may have convinced yourself you will never understand how to work it, no matter how many times you are shown, and lo and behold – you still don't. Or if you believe that most people are unfriendly you are likely to express this in your manner when you interact through your subtle hostility, and people will likely respond in a way that then supports your beliefs. Or you may say, "I always drop things" or "I can't ever remember names." These are unhelpful and unnecessary at best, and they will make you nervous about doing these things, create physical tension and divert your attention so that you will be more likely to do them. This reinforces your belief and the cycle continues and becomes stronger.

> *Years of thinking certain thoughts, and then feeling the same way, and then thinking equal to those feelings . . . creates a memorized state of being in which we can emphatically declare our I am statement as an absolute. That means we're now at the point when we define ourselves as this state of being. Our thoughts and feelings have merged.*
>
> Joe Dispenza

From Joe Dispenza, 2012, *Breaking the Habit of Being Yourself.* Reprinted with permission.

We limit ourselves and our world with labels and words. For example, I am disabled, I am sick, I am tired, this is terrible, I am depressed, I am shy, I am a terrible dancer, I am. . . . Is that really who you are and all you can do? Those affirmations are unlikely to make you feel good and optimistic and ready to embrace life's challenges. So what would happen if you didn't have those thoughts? What would happen if you had positive and encouraging thoughts instead? As Anthony De Mello (1990) writes, "The point is that most of what we feel and think we conjure up for ourselves in our heads."

Affirmations are just words, but words are extremely powerful and you need to use them carefully.

What is the purpose of affirmations?

The purpose of affirmations is to create conscious thoughts that help you, so that your life is not dominated, dictated and determined by affirmations that prevent you from living the life you want, enjoying inner peace, enjoying your experience of life and achieving your goals. You are using your mind as the tool it is – *for* you, and in the process you break the cycle of negativity.

> ❝ *When you think optimistically you'll feel more confident, more relaxed, and happier all round.* ❞
>
> Daniel Freeman and Jason Freeman

From Freeman and Freeman, 2012, *You Can Be Happy*. Reprinted with permission.

Affirmations can act as reminders – to keep you mindful, as Thich Nhat Hanh (2014) encourages, for example, "Breathing in, I'm aware of my whole body"; to reassure you – for example, so you remember you don't need to worry, the situation you face can be handled (when in a panic you forget you had come to a resolution about how you were managing it e.g. "I just need to observe and connect with my body" as I listen to the interview questions); and to keep your mind space a nice place to be ("I experience my inner space as a safe haven.").

Affirmations can also be used to increase motivation and improve performance in therapy, increase self-love and self-belief, improve attention, and overcome fears. They can help to quieten and overpower the voice of the "critical parent" (see chapter: "The Voice in Your Head") and they can bring about a calm state of mind.

There are some people who will say positive thinking can be negative, as it sets you up to focus on what you don't have and it doesn't work anyway. But this is more in relation to achieving and getting material things in the future and about external situations that you have less control over. Affirmations used in the way intended here focus on the present and in particular your attitude and your approach to it. It is not trying to deny reality but to change your reactions to it and how you handle situations – which are all within your inner self and which you do have power over. They in effect influence your mind-set on a conscious and subconscious level. If you are positive and enthusiastic and are willing to give things a go, you are more likely to achieve material goals anyway. But this is really about focusing on the inner self. It is simply about freeing yourself from the negative self-talk and opening you up to your true potential.

> *Thoughts influence how we behave, what we choose to do and not do, and the quality of our performance.*
>
> Dennis Greenberger and Christine A. Padesky

From Dennis Greenberger and Christine A. Padesky, 1995, *Mind over Mood,* p. 25. Reprinted with permission.

The affirmations your client has will set the tone for the therapy session and significantly impact on the outcome. But you can choose to promote a positive attitude to what you do and so can your clients.

How do affirmations work?

"When we say something over and over again, we create neural connections in our brain. The more we say it, the more connections we create and the stronger they become" (Hamilton, 2008). This is possible due to the plasticity of the brain; you can change the physiology, create new wiring and rewire the brain (see chapter: "The Power of the Mind"). We are not set in stone unless we believe we are ("a leopard doesn't change its spots"; this is who I am and that's that). We have the capacity to change and in doing so we change our lives.

To rewire the brain requires repetition, repetition, repetition. Our thinking and behaviour changes the brain – they are the tools we have. Select your thoughts and behaviours and repeat, repeat, repeat!

You need at the same time to be aware that you are likely affirming the opposite to what you want whilst you are still changing your thoughts (when you are not paying attention to them). You will need to balance these with your chosen affirmations – therefore you will need to do more of them to start off with.

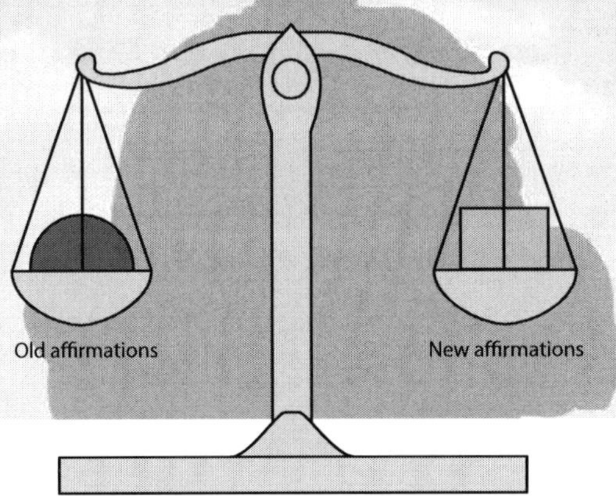

Figure 10.1 Old affirmations versus new affirmations – tip the balance

How to create affirmations

> *How do you feel right now? Do you feel good?
> Do you feel bad? . . . Would you like to feel better?
> Then reach for a better feeling thought.*
>
> *Louise L. Hay*

From Louise Hay, 2004, *I Can Do It*. Reprinted with permission.

Become aware of your thinking and decide what you want to think and how you want to change your attitudes, your reactions and your behaviours. Do you want to be more positive?

Once you have decided you need to think about the wording of your affirmations. They need to be said in the present tense, as "Affirmations influence our unconscious, where only the present exists" (Houel with Godefroy, 1994). For example:

"I am fully focused in therapy sessions", rather than "I will be fully focused in the next therapy session". It will always be something that happens in the future if you use the future tense.

Always say what you do want, not what you're trying to avoid. For example, "I am calm and serene in this situation", rather than "I am not afraid in this situation", as your subconscious will focus more on the word "afraid" (which is powerful because of the emotions it conjures up) than "not".

How to use affirmations

A lot and with gusto!

Affirmations can be used throughout the day, and throughout your life. It is essential to make the effort if you want to take responsibility for your life. Negative affirmations typically overpower positive ones "because there are more of them and they're usually said with great feeling" (Hay, 2004), so you need to put in the same level of feeling (or more) with the positive affirmations and try to make them outnumber the negative ones. If you aim for 1,000 repetitions a day you will be entering into the spirit of doing affirmations without needing to keep a tally.

It does take effort; it means thinking consciously. But you will be rewarded with life experiences that you feel confident and comfortable in.

Summary

- Affirmations are our thoughts and beliefs.

- Affirmations are powerful and help to create our life experience.

- Affirmations can be used by clients to optimise therapy outcomes.

Activity

With your client, go through the suggested affirmations that may be appropriate for them and/or encourage them to make up their own.

Identify times to practise to make them part of your client's routine or help deal with certain situations. Go through ways of how they can remind themselves to do this, e.g. leave post-it notes around the house, engrave a bracelet, write any affirmations they think of in a notebook kept to hand for the purpose, or keep affirmation cards in their wallet. They can even sing or chant them.

Possible affirmations

I can do it!
I can handle any situation.
I can depend on myself.
Peace is inside me at all times.
I am not my thoughts.
Nothing bothers me.
I am kind and gentle with myself, and treat myself as a friend.
I choose what I want to focus on.
I know I can choose drama or bliss.
I consciously create my life.
I welcome nothingness: space and silence.
My primary focus is on my inner self.
I know nothing of suffering.
I can be happy in my stress and tension.

Mindfulness affirmations

I go beyond my mind and I observe.
I watch my thoughts to calm my mind.
I am observing.
I am listening.
I am aware of what I am doing.
I relax into the moment.

I notice everything around me.
I am in touch with my body and inner self and I am listening.
I am aware of how I am feeling.
I welcome and am curious about every moment.
I am aware of the room I am in.

References

De Mello, Anthony. 1990. *Awareness*. Grand Rapids, MI: Fount Paperbacks.

Dispenza, Joe. 2012. *Breaking the Habit of Being Yourself*. Carlsbad, CA: Hay House Inc.

Freeman, Daniel. Professor and Freeman, Jason. 2012. *You Can Be Happy*, p. 77. Harlow: Pearson Education Limited. © Daniel Freeman and Jason Freeman 2012.

Greenberger, Dennis and Padesky, Christine A. 1995. *Mind over Mood*. New York, NY: The Guildford Press.

Hamilton, David R. PhD. 2008. *How Your Mind Can Heal Your Body*. London: Hay House UK Ltd.

Hay, Louise L. 2004. *I Can Do It*. Carlsbad, CA: Hay House Inc.

Houel, Alan and Godefroy, Christian. 1994. *How to Cope with Difficult People*. London: Sheldon Press.

Nhat Hanh, Thich. 2014. *Peace of Mind*. London: Bantam Press.

11. The body, posture and movement

The mind-body connection

> **"Over time, our persistent mental attitudes become fixed in our muscles (a habit of thought becomes a habit of posture)."**
>
> *Mike George*

From Mike George, 1998, *Learn to Relax*, reproduced with permission.

Aims of the chapter

- For the client to think about their body, and learn that how they use it can affect the way they feel.

- To learn to use the body in a way that supports mental and physical health.

Mind-body connection

The mind and body are both continuously sharing emotional information with each other.

Your thoughts and emotions affect your whole body; they are connected. It is impossible to consider them separately, "emotion is literally smeared throughout the body . . . in your brain chemistry, your autonomic nervous system and your muscles" (Hamilton, 2015). When you are stressed for example because of a deadline, your body feels that stress. When you feel happy and confident, this is reflected in your posture and facial expression – you hold yourself up more, shoulders back, looking ahead or up, and you smile. If you are feeling low you do the opposite – you slouch, look down and may frown or pull a grimace. It is automatic; the body follows the emotions – just consider a sports person who has

Figure 11.1 Good posture and positive energy demonstrated after winning a race

just won their event – notice the positive energy that takes hold of their body in response to their feelings of elation; any inhibitions are forgotten as their powerful emotions are engaged.

The body is extremely responsive to flashes of emotions that we constantly experience. Over time the body can develop health issues that reflect the stresses that you have been feeling and not letting go of, e.g. heart disease, eczema, psoriasis and hair loss, to name just a few. What you think really does affect your body (see chapter: "The Power of the Mind"). An event/experience which produces a significant stress response can be perceived as a traumatic experience. This is not limited to that experienced by war veterans or other life-endangering situations (known as Trauma with a big T), but can also be produced by more everyday traumas (known as trauma with a little t). That is to say trauma is personal to the individual and a matter of perception. This reportedly results in trapped energy in the body, which can be stored there long term. As Peter Levine (1997) writes, traumatic symptoms "stem from the frozen residue of energy that has not been resolved and discharged; this residue remains trapped in the nervous system where it can wreak havoc on our bodies and spirits." Physically moving such as when fleeing a dangerous situation helps to release this energy, according to Worby (2015), "In animals shaking would naturally be seen after such an event," which would resolve this, but such physical release behaviours are not always possible or socially acceptable for us. In his book Waking the Tiger (1997) Levine describes another method to discharge this energy through the "felt sense" or "focusing" (first described by Eugene Gendlin in his book *Focusing*), which requires tuning into all that ". . . you feel and know about the given subject at a given time . . . [the felt sense] . . . encompasses it and communicates it to you all at once rather than detail by detail" (Gendlin, 2003). By focusing on the felt sense shifts in feelings/energy can occur gradually and naturally, and frozen energy from trauma can be discharged. Please refer to these books for further information on this.

> *Continuous modes of thinking and speaking produce body behaviors and postures and 'eases' or dis-eases. . . . Older people's faces and bodies show so clearly a life-time of thinking patterns.*
>
> Louise L. Hay

From Louise Hay, 1984, *You Can Heal Your Life*. Reprinted with permission.

However, the flipside is that how you use your body affects your thought and emotions. For example, frowning and slouching depress the mood and sitting or standing upright and smiling elevate the mood. It doesn't even matter that you don't feel that way initially because "even an artificially induced frown or smile tends to induce the corresponding emotions of anger or happiness" (Dalai Lama and Cutler, 1999).

This two-way process can lead to vicious cycles – you feel stressed, so then you start breathing rapidly and shallowly (hyperventilating), and your muscles start tensing up. But in response to these uncomfortable and possibly alarming feelings you feel more stressed, which then increases the symptoms of stress in your body . . . the cycle goes on until we remove ourselves from the situation, distract ourselves or manage to "pep talk" using positive affirmations ourselves back down to a more calm state – or become mindful of what is happening.

According to Mark Williams and Danny Penman (2011) "research is showing us that our whole outlook on life can be shifted by tiny changes in the body." So you can choose to feel stressed by adopting certain postures to reflect this and encourage these feelings, or you can encourage what David Hamilton (2015) describes as a "virtuous cycle." You can position yourself in a way that demonstrates happiness and confidence or any other emotion that you prefer to feel. These postures will feed back to your mind a positive feeling and will encourage the corresponding emotions . . . the cycle can continue.

> *Moving our body can produce the feelings we want to produce.*
>
> David R. Hamilton

From David R. Hamilton, 2015, *I Heart Me*. Reprinted with permission.

Move and hold your body in a way that is associated with the positive emotions you want to feel. Smile and laugh for no reason.

The body as a communicator

> **The body is always talking to us, if we will only take the time to listen.**
>
> *Louise L. Hay*

From Louise Hay, 1984, *You Can Heal Your Life*. Reprinted with permission.

You just have to do some people-watching to start noticing how most people do not have ideal postures which reflect a sense of ease within them. Observe clients particularly – many will have rounded shoulders and sit slumped in the chair. Their posture is communicating feelings of stress and tension, worries and dissatisfaction with themselves and with their life.

The body is always reflecting and communicating important messages that we need to tune into to be comfortable in it and enjoy good health. It is all too common though to completely ignore our bodies. "We can easily spend so much time 'in our head' that we almost forget we have a body at all" (Williams and Penman, 2011). But if we keep ignoring the body, it just turns up the volume and we experience more symptoms and to a more distressing degree, until the body finally has our full attention.

Mindfulness and the body

Living more fully in our bodies helps connect us to the here and now.

Babies and small children instinctively adopt postures that are good for their health and well-being. But then as we get older we adopt postural habits and facial expressions which are less healthy, partly because those around us adopt the same postures – we unconsciously mimic those around us. Furthermore, the trials of life can affect how we position ourselves (how we have learnt to physically respond to life) – if we learn to become fearful we learn to make ourselves physically smaller. Also, our lifestyle contributes to the way we hold ourselves – most of us sit for longer periods of time than is healthy. We are creatures of movement; we need to move. However, as our bad habits become hard-wired into the brain they become automatic and even feel and appear normal. The person who sits with good posture is more likely to stand out.

Take control by becoming aware

Being constantly mindful of your body (aware of the position and movement of the parts of the body – proprioception and kinaesthesia, and the sensations throughout) allows you to turn your attention inwards more and listen to your body, and to be aware of the messages it is sending you and the messages you are giving out because of your body language (do you really want to give those messages out?). This awareness can naturally allow changes to occur that are beneficial for your overall health and well-being or you can take active control to make changes, or you can do both.

Connecting with the body

Get out of your mind and into your body.

How disconnected are you from your body? Can you sense it at all? Do you feel you have much control over it? Are you prone to having "accidents"? As babies and young children we connect with the world through our bodies more, and as we get older we connect more through our minds. Through practising mindfulness you can learn to reconnect with your body, but it will take time.

By reconnecting with your body you are once again fully in it and experiencing it; you will inhabit your body. By doing this you can align your body with your mind and the essence that you are – your inner self; the marrying of your physical form with the formless aspect of yourself. The physical form, which has its own intelligence, can then freely communicate with your mind.

Make friends with your body and it will guide you.

If you are in your body and taking the time to experience it, this will help increase your appreciation for it and help you develop a better relationship with it. Allowing time to place your attention on your body will allow you to reflect on all the amazing things your body does for you, without you having to do anything. It will reduce your stress over trivial aspects of your appearance that you are dissatisfied with and make you more grateful to have the body that you have. You can see it as the remarkable vehicle it is that has been loaned to you for this life. It is the most important thing we will ever "possess", and normally we just take it completely for granted. Having this genuine insight will automatically make you want to look after your body, explore its capabilities more, use it more, and marvel at it. It will also make you more connected to the way you use it and the activities you engage in. All this awareness contributes to lowering stress levels and reducing tension in the body.

Be in your body, listen to it, appreciate it and treat it with respect; it is amazing.

Actively working on posture

> **We can consciously use our body to change how we feel about ourselves. In my experience, it's actually about the fastest way to change how you feel at any given moment.**
>
> *David R. Hamilton*

From David R. Hamilton, 2015, *I Heart Me*. Reprinted with permission.

Once you know that how you hold your body influences your thoughts and emotions, you can then do something about it – you now have more control. I don't think anyone wants to feel listless or ill at ease, so try sitting in such a way that your body demonstrates an attitude of presence, of peace, of contentment and confidence . . . the posture feeds the attitude, and the attitude feeds the posture. Visualise someone who exudes the emotions that you would like to experience, imagine yourself doing the same and do it for yourself. David Hamilton (2015) recommends emulating Wonder Woman, whilst Jon Kabat-Zinn in his book *Wherever You Go There You Are* (2004) encourages bringing into your posture and attitude the qualities of a mountain –

elevation . . . [and] massiveness. . . . When you sit with strong intentionality, the body itself makes a statement of deep conviction and commitment in its carriage. These radiate inward and outward. A dignified sitting posture is itself an affirmation of freedom.

You can also think Shakespearian actor or ballerina, or a singer known for belting such as Shirley Bassey or an opera singer. The aim is to expand and extend your body – get bigger. Move into the space around you that is just waiting to be used; explore it. It is

Figure 11.2 Young children running with abandon

Figure 11.3 A young child laughing with hilarity

through the nothingness of space that we are made aware of the tangible, physical forms that exist within it, just as the nothingness of silence allows us to be aware of noise. Enjoy the space. Don't just focus on keeping a good posture and freezing it, staying locked into position. Good posture needs to be incorporated into movements. We are meant to move.

Practice

It takes practice to have this level of self-control when suddenly confronted with an extremely stressful situation. But you can learn to "embody dignity, stillness, an unwavering equanimity in the face of any mind state which presents itself" (Williams and Penman, 2011).

Working on your own posture

Posture and facial expression are infectious. If you, as the therapist, can become aware of your own, you will be more able to alter these as needed with clients to reflect your attentiveness and care, and also encourage positivity and energy when appropriate.

Posture and attention

Good posture promotes positive, attentive energy.

Improving your posture not only changes how you feel, but can also improve your ability to attend to the here and now both within you and outside of you (mindfulness). It connects you to this moment. With an upright posture you are in a state of alert readiness in the now. You are wide awake and open to the moment and what is required of you; you are ready to give of yourself, which means your client in this position will be more ready and attentive to therapy.

Opening up and expanding the physical self automatically hones your attention. Be aware of all your muscles, particularly the back, shoulders, neck and eyes. Keep them in the optimum positions and take control of your eyes. In this fast-paced society where we are bombarded with stimuli and come across dozens, possibly hundreds, or even thousands of people in a day, scanning items in shops, perhaps scrutinising labels under harsh lights, and then staring at quick moving images on screens for extended periods, it can feel overwhelming for our eyes and we end up shrinking from paying full attention to what is around us. Don't allow your eyes to be taken for a ride without your knowledge and allow them regular relaxation.

Adopting a relaxed but alert and upright posture helps sustain focus.

Summary

- The mind and body are connected – your thoughts and emotions affect your body and posture, but your posture also affects your thoughts and emotions.

- Through mindfulness practice we can become more aware of our bodies and postures and what they are communicating. We are then able to respond to these messages.

- Adopting an upright posture helps with attention; this is needed for mindfulness and for optimum participation in therapy sessions.

Activities

- Tune in to how you are feeling in your body. Be mindful of your own posture and facial expressions. What do they say about you?

- Observe your client's posture and facial expressions – what are they communicating about how they feel?

- Ask the client to sit or stand in a way that communicates confidence and as if they have no worries. Perhaps they can imagine themselves as a person who reflects these attributes the most, such as a barrister in a court of law arguing a case, or a performer in the West End or on Broadway, or perhaps even as the prime minister. Encourage the client to be aware of their whole body, including their shoulders, neck, chin and eyes. Do this with them to help alleviate any self-consciousness. Ask them to observe any changes in how they feel.

- Feel and connect to the inner body: Ask the client to close their eyes. Ask them to feel the energy – or any sensations they notice in one of their hands. Allow them to feel it for a few moments before, asking them to focus on the energy in the other hand. Now allow them to focus on their arms, then the feet, the legs, the stomach, and then the chest. Now allow them to feel the energy in all these parts of the body at the same time. Allow several moments for each part of the body and then for all these parts.

- Tensing and relaxing: Talk your client though each part of the body starting with the face. Encourage the client to tense each muscle for several moments before then allowing it to relax.

- Massage: As a speech therapist I was encouraged to offer shoulder massages to voice clients with muscle-tension dysphonia. If you feel this is appropriate you can offer a gentle shoulder massage. It can also give you more of an idea about just how tense your client is.

- Gentle stretching of the shoulders and neck

Other activities that can be recommended to clients to help them connect with and move their body for physical and emotional well-being

- Mindfulness of body and breath

- Mindful walking meditation

- Stretching. Face stretches – funny faces. Humour here is helpful.

- Laughter yoga

- Suitable exercise

- Swinging/float around the room (see chapter: "The Breath" – this can be done without coordinating the breath)

- Alexander technique

- The Feldenkrais Method

- Tai Chi

- Yoga

- Pilates

- Qi Gong

- Osteopathy/chiropractic treatment – to release tensions to improve posture and allow the body to function better

- Grounding/Earthing. This allows you to benefit from the Earth's energy – emerging research is showing that this can help with many conditions including stress and tension. Walk or run barefoot outside on the grass. Being in the sea has the same effect.

- Open water swimming. Not for everyone as this can be very cold, but research shows this can be very good for mental health.

- Eye exercises. See description of 'palming' in Visualisation chapter.

- Massage. Client can do this themselves, e.g. the neck and face, or they could visit a spa and enjoy a massage by a professional.

- Dance. Feel the music – let it literally move you. Client can do this alone at home or out in a club or group.

- Shoulder dance

- Run on the spot, bring knees up if able, and listen to music to help keep up the momentum. You then don't need to go out and you don't need much space.

- Move about with abandon like a child, e.g. run around flying – flap wings like a child – chest out.

- Pretend to conduct a piece of classical music – beware of using some "relaxing" classical music, as it can sound more depressing than relaxing to some people.

- Do anything that makes you laugh, e.g. watch comedies, go to a laughter group.

- Hug!

- Exchange the energy! Shake it up/relieve the tension – movement. Humans need to move. Release pent up energy – let it flow.

Note: These can all be visualised if your client can't physically do them (see chapter: "The Power of the Mind").

References

Gendlin, Eugene T. 2003. *Focusing*. Rider Books. London.

George, Mike. 1998. *Learn to Relax*. London: Duncan Baird Publishers.

Hamilton, David R. PhD. 2015. *I Heart Me*. London: Hay House UK Ltd.

Hay, Louise L. 1984. *You Can Heal Your Life*. Carlsbad, CA: Hay House Inc.

HH Dalai Lama and Cutler, Howard C. 1999. *The Art of Happiness*. New York: Penguin.

Kabat-Zinn, Jon. 2004. *Wherever You Go There You Are*. London: Piatkus Books.

Levine, Peter A. with Ann Frederick. 1997. *Waking the Tiger*. Berkeley, CA: North Atlantic Books.

Rome, David and Martin, Hope. 2011. Are You Listening? In Barry Boyce (ed.), *The Mindfulness Revolution*. Boston, MA: Shambhala Publications Inc., pp. 211–218.

Schneider, Meir. 2012. *Vision for Life: Ten Steps to Natural Eyesight Improvement*. Berkeley, CA: North Atlantic Books.

Williams, Mark and Penman, Danny. 2011. *Mindfulness*. London: Piatkus.

Worby, Patricia. 2015. *The Scar That Won't Heal*. CreateSpace Independent Publishing Forum.

12. The breath

From James D'Angelo, 2005, *The Healing Power of the Human Voice*. Reprinted with permission of publisher.

Aims

- To learn about the benefits of clients' improved awareness of their breathing.

- To understand about the connection of the breath to stress and tension.

- To learn and use techniques to improve breathing habits.

Obstacles to healthy breathing

We are all born with healthy breathing patterns; it comes naturally because it is hard-wired. Unfortunately this pattern slowly and steadily gives way to unhealthy habits. This happens for a variety of reasons – physical, environmental and emotional (such as stress), but also excessive talking, lack of physical exercise, stuffy environments, poor diet and a belief that taking big breaths is beneficial. The process is so gradual that we are not always conscious of this transition.

Negative emotions and the breath

Breathing pattern disorders, which include chronic hyperventilation (breathing in excess of normal metabolic requirements), oral breathing, rapid and predominantly upper chest breathing, and also irregular breathing, typically become the norm as we go through life, and we lose the "nose-belly" (Bradley and Clifton-Smith, 2003) healthy breathing pattern of infancy. According to Patrick McKeown in his book *Anxiety Free* (2010), stress, anxiety and anger are commonly the root cause of breathing pattern disorders in adulthood.

Chronic stress can cause chronic hyperventilation, and acute stress can cause acute episodes of hyperventilation, to the point of a panic attack. The stress response and breath are interconnected, with stress and anxiety causing breathing pattern disorders and breathing pattern disorders increasing stress levels.

Carbon dioxide and the Bohr Effect

Healthy breathing is important to maintain an appropriate balance of oxygen and carbon dioxide. The catalyst for the release of oxygen from the red blood cells to the tissues is carbon dioxide. Habitually breathing a volume of air greater than what the body needs removes too much carbon dioxide from the blood through the lungs. The lowering of carbon dioxide from the blood increases blood pH, resulting in the bond between oxygen and the blood becoming tighter. In addition, the carotid arteries, which supply the brain with blood flow and oxygen, constrict. The combined result from breathing too much air is reduced blood flow and oxygen delivery to the brain. When we hyperventilate, then, we lose too much carbon dioxide. Hyperventilation starves "your body of oxygen [as it is not released and is unable to be used] . . . Your brain is being starved, contributing to anxiety, depression and stress" (McKeown, 2010). The stress you subsequently experience then increases your rate of breathing. The cycle continues and intensifies.

Mouth breathing and poor posture

Mouth breathing and poor posture also contribute to chronic hyperventilation. Healthy and efficient breathing takes place through the nose. The nose plays an important role in breathing as it reduces the airflow by creating more resistance, it also warms and sterilises incoming air, helps keep airways open and, compared to mouth breathing, improves arterial oxygen uptake and delivery to the cells. Nose breathing slows down breathing, helping to activate the body's relaxation response. Posture is also key to good breathing, as you are able to use your muscles effectively for diaphragmatic breathing if your whole body is in a comfortable, relaxed position, allowing for free and unconstrained movement of the muscles so that they can be used fully.

Once unhealthy breathing habits are developed, they may feel normal. We can usually take breathing for granted – one of those unconscious functions of our body that we can ignore, that we don't have to think about because it just happens – so we are unaware of how we are breathing and that it is not flowing smoothly, freely – in and out. We also may assume that we have no power to control our breath, it is something that happens to us, and we have to just let it, and perhaps we even live in fear of it, never knowing when it is going to suddenly take us over, gripping us with its power.

However, there are things we can do to work on our breathing, and it is important we understand this and make efforts to do this to contribute to our mental and physical health.

Benefits of healthy breathing

The main benefits of healthy breathing we are considering here are the reduction of stress, tension and anxiety, as well as improved sleep (which is very important to help with anxiety) and energy levels. However, there are many health benefits for our whole body when we work on developing healthy breathing patterns – all bodily functions depend on our breath to keep oxygen and carbon dioxide levels at a healthy ratio to work as effectively as possible. Knowing this can help increase a client's motivation to engage with breathing exercises in sessions and also continue them independently between sessions.

> 66 *There is a direct connection between quality of breathing and inner calm.* 99
>
> Mike George

From Mike George, 2003, *Learn to Find Inner Peace reprinted with permission.*

Working on the breath helps reduce stress and tension in two ways – firstly it improves oxygenation of the brain, allowing it to function properly and to think calmly and clearly. Due to the Bohr Effect, overbreathing and the resulting lack of oxygen in the brain causes abnormally increased activity, to the point of being "out of control", as a result of the appearance of "spontaneous and asynchronous ('self-generated') thoughts . . . [however] . . . The brain by regulating breathing, controls its own excitability" (Balestrino and Somjen as cited in Rakhimov, 2014).

Hyperventilation can lead to feelings of anxiety and panic, but feelings of anxiety and panic can lead to hyperventilation. This can lead to a vicious cycle, and a feeling of helplessness and a sense of being out of control. But by controlling the breath you can reduce feelings of panic – the cycle begins to reverse.

Secondly, focusing on the breath redirects the attention away from thoughts (which cause stress) and take it to the body. This is another mindfulness technique which allows you to still your mind, to break the cycle of compulsive thinking and be alert in the here and now. With your attention on the breath and not the internal chatter, you are released from the prison of your mind and are free to experience the joy of being, and to enjoy the peace of the present moment.

Another significant benefit of breathing well is increased energy. According to Dinah Bradley and Tania Clifton-Smith (2003), using your diaphragm and abdominal muscles appropriately uses up just 2–4 per cent of your available energy, whereas upper chest breathing "gobbles up" 10 per cent! Patrick McKeown (2010) also asserts that nose breathing activates the diaphragm whereas mouth breathing activates the upper chest. Try it and see; take a big breath through your mouth and observe what part of your body moves. In addition, breathing through the nose harnesses the gas nitric oxide to improve the distribution of blood throughout the lungs to enable a better gas exchange to take place. Ultimately, "diaphragmatic breathing is more efficient because the air is drawn deeper into the lungs, amount of blood flow in the lower lobes of the lungs is greater than in the upper" (McKeown, 2010). This results in more oxygenation of the blood and reduces the loss of carbon dioxide. With increased energy your client will be better able to engage in therapy.

Types of breathing techniques

The mind, emotions and breath are all connected. You can consciously change your breathing to control your emotions.

These are some of the widely used breathing techniques:

- **Nose-breathing versus mouth-breathing**

Nose-breathing is important for healthy breathing; however, many people are in the habit of mouth-breathing and may not be aware of it – it may be something they have been doing for years and has become hard-wired. It is important when working on the breath for your client to first become aware if this is the case for them. As is the case for all habits, it can take time to change back to nose-breathing. But it is worth encouraging your client to persevere and find ways of reminding themselves, such as with using post-it notes around the house or asking friends and family members to remind them.

- **Mindful breathing**

This in essence is mindfulness of breath – simply watching it. Eckhart Tolle writes about this in *A New Earth* (2006), "Be aware of your breathing as often as you are able, whenever you remember. Do that for one year, and it will be more powerfully transformative than attending all these [inner development] courses. And it's free." It may sound too simple but it is effective and can be tricky keeping your focus and suspending any judgements about it. You may find your breath shallow and irregular, and this new awareness can cause unease or even panic initially. With mindfulness you stay with whatever you observe, even if it feels worse. The more you stay with it, the healthier your breathing pattern will become.

- **Deep/diaphragmatic/abdominal breathing**

This breathing technique is actually the way we were born to breathe for most of the day (breathing naturally changes during vigorous physical exercise) – just watch how a baby breathes. It is the most healthy and effective way to breathe, and what many of us have lost. The diaphragm is the key breathing muscle and if we do not do deep, abdominal breathing, we lose the ability to breathe down to it and work the muscle. This is made harder due to stress and the subsequent tension we then feel in the tummy, which inhibits the movement of the diaphragm.

Buteyko Technique

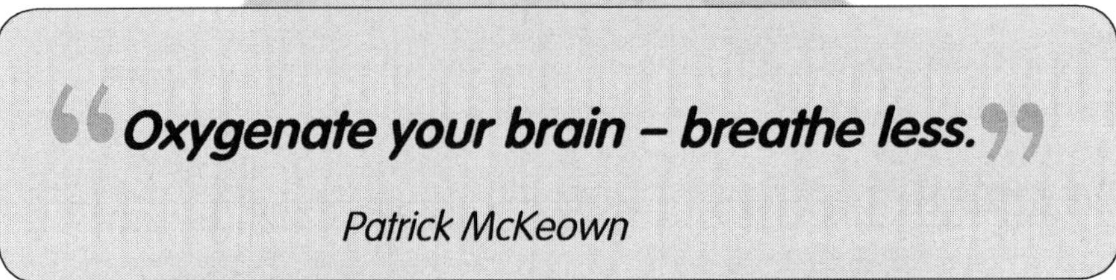

From Patrick McKeown, 2010, *Anxiety Free.* Reprinted with permission.

The Buteyko Technique encourages deep but light breathing. It focuses on reducing the amount of air you breathe – slowing your breathing and creating a non-stressful need for air, to consciously ensure that you are breathing an appropriate volume of air. Once this has been practised, it is then combined with diaphragmatic breathing.

The technique can be used for specific points during the day, e.g. to curb anxiety when going for a job interview, but also can be used at times throughout every day.

- **Yoga and breathing**

According to Fiona Agombar in her book *Beat Fatigue with Yoga* (2002), "In yoga, it is thought that we are allocated a set number of breaths, so that life is measured in breaths rather than years. Therefore, it is thought that slowing down your breath will help increase your life span." There are many different breathing exercises in yoga aimed at reducing breathing rate through breath retention; there are therefore similarities to the Buteyko Technique. They can facilitate deep relaxation, help with overall health and increase energy.

Summary

- The breath and the stress response are interconnected – stress causes hyperventilation, and hyperventilation causes stress.

- Hyperventilation starves the brain and body of oxygen.

- Healthy breathing habits help reduce stress and increase energy.

- There are various breathing techniques and exercises to help promote healthy breathing habits.

Activities

When doing any of these exercises with a client encourage them to listen to their body. Begin slowly and gently, don't force anything and stop if the client begins to feel unwell. Start with short practices and build up to 10 minutes.

Whilst breathing exercises are safe for most people, it is worth asking your client to check with their GP first as it may be contraindicated with certain conditions, such as epilepsy, type 1 diabetes, high blood pressure and heart conditions.

Mindful breathing

- Meditation:

  "Sit up straight in a comfortable position and close your eyes. Start to be aware of your breath, make sure you are breathing through your nose if you can but otherwise resist the urge to try to control it. Be aware of any judgements you may have of your breathing or any reactions you are experiencing in response to it. Be aware of your reaction and the breath, but carry on letting the breath happen, simply witnessing it, not trying to control it in any way. Let transformation occur naturally in its own time. Feel the air coming through your nostrils. Past the tips of your nostrils. Notice the difference between how it feels when you are breathing in and when you are breathing out. Follow the breath in – feel your body as you inhale – your neck and shoulders, your chest and your tummy. Don't try to control your muscles, just be aware of them. Do the same as you are breathing out – feel the muscles in your body, the movements. Keep watching attentively. Breathing in, and breathing out. No pressure to breathe in any particular way. You may or may not notice changes in the rhythm of the breath, the movement of your body, the muscles. There is no need to worry about it being right or wrong, the benefits come from just watching and allowing your body to do what it is doing. Enjoy breathing in, and breathing out. Do this for a few moments . . .

  [Allow client a few minutes to do this]. "Now become aware of the chair you are sitting on. Be aware of any sounds you can hear. When you are ready open your eyes."

- Mindful breathing and relaxing the ears. This exercise is recommended by Meir Schneider in his book *Vision for Life: Ten Steps to Natural Eyesight Improvement* (2012), in which he emphasises relaxation. Put your thumbs into your ears and listen to your breath. Listen carefully. How does it sound? Like ocean waves or the wind perhaps? Breathe deeply and slowly.

Diaphragmatic breathing

Teach your client to breathe down to the tummy, rather than just in the chest:

- One way of developing this way of breathing is described by Dinah Bradley and Tania Clifton-Smith in their book *Breathing Works for Asthma* (2003) – Ask your client to put their hands on top of their head and close their eyes. This position makes it harder to breathe from the chest. Encourage the client to allow for the slight pause at the end of the out-breath, and let the in-breath occur naturally on its own. Breathe out fully. When the client starts to be aware of their tummy expanding on the in-breath they can gradually lower their arms. See if they can now continue the deeper breathing. If not try again.

- Another way to practise diaphragmatic breathing is by having the client lie down and the feel their stomach with their hand, or they can place a small bag of rice or something similar on their stomach. The client watches and/or feels the stomach moving as they breathe. Then they can do the same on the chest – there should be no movement. This can be practised sitting upright with the placing of the hand.

- To help activate the diaphragm further the client can practise lying or sitting whilst gently pushing the stomach out (client to keep their hand on the stomach). Then they can gently draw the stomach in. No need to think about the breath doing this.

- The above exercise can then be combined with breathing:

Breathe in, and gently push the stomach out. Breathe out and gently pull your stomach in. Encourage the client to relax the shoulders. Remind them to minimise chest movements. Point out that they need to be aware of not allowing the stomach to get too big – this may cause dizziness.

These are exercises the client may have to practise a lot by themselves between sessions.

Buteyko Technique

Many small breath holds – an exercise to stop panic attacks, stress and anxiety – is recommended by Patrick McKeown in *Anxiety Free* (2010):

Breathe in and out then hold the breath for 2 seconds. Client needs to feel a tolerable shortage of air. If comfortable this can be extended to up to 5 seconds. Breathe normally for 10–15 seconds then, when you next breathe out, hold the breath again for 2 seconds. This can be practised for as long as the client wants/needs (throughout the day even) and will help them to feel calmer.

Reducing the breath can be incorporated into everyday life as an informal practice in this way. If you are interested in using the technique further, it is worth buying a book purely about this or consulting a practitioner.

Yogic breathing exercises

- *The Square*

Breathe in for a count of four, hold your breath for a count of four, breathe out for a count of four and then hold your breath for a count of four (4:4:4:4). This can be increased to 6:6:6:6.

- *Alternate nostril breathing*

The above square breathing exercise can also be used with this exercise. Start by exhaling through both nostrils. Then block your right nostril with your thumb and inhale through the left nostril (to a count of four – as slowly as you can). Now block the left nostril and exhale through the right in the same way (same duration/rhythm) as you just breathed in. Then inhale through the right nostril, block it, and exhale through your left. Continue this for up to one minute initially. You can gradually increase the length of practice, but make sure the slow, even rhythm is maintained throughout.

Swinging

If you have room, perhaps with a group, you can have clients try moving around the room whilst swinging their arms and bending the knees. It can be done to music. A version of this exercise is described in Patsy Rodenburg's book *Presence* (2007), but it is also an exercise I practised and enjoyed on a course organised by the British Voice Association:

Ask the client to stand with one arm up behind them and one arm up in front of them. As the client takes a step they gently bend their knees as much as they are able – if at all. At the same time the arms come down, and cross over – one arm goes up behind them, and the other goes up in front of them. Move around the room in this way for a few minutes. Once mastered ask the client to coordinate their movements with the breath. So when they are holding their arms up, pause and feel the suspension of the breath.

This exercise helps to make clients present and relaxed, and allows the breath and energy in them to flow freely.

Visualisation and colour

- Visualise breathing in a particular colour (see chapter on visualisation for benefits of colour therapy). Any colour you are drawn to will work. Observe the colour going in, and going out. Watch and see if it changes at all.

- Meir Schneider (2012) recommends visualising your whole body expanding as you breathe in and shrinking as you breathe out.

Laughter yoga

You may want to encourage your client to attend a laughter yoga group – or perhaps try it for yourself first! Lesley Lyle in her book *Laugh Your Way to Happiness* (2014) states, "Laughter yoga is particularly beneficial as it exercises the diaphragm, encourages us to breathe deeply and clears stale residual air from our lungs. One of the reasons people feel invigorated after laughter yoga is because of an increase in oxygen that goes straight to their brain, making them feel energetic and revitalized."

Physical exercise

A moving muscle produces more carbon dioxide, therefore encouraging your client to exercise is also important for a healthy balance of oxygen and carbon dioxide.

References

Agombar, Fiona. 2002. *Beat Fatigue with Yoga*. London: Thorsons.

Bradley, Dinah and Clifton-Smith, Tania. 2003. *Breathing Works for Asthma*. London: Kyle Cathie Limited.

D'Angelo, James. PhD. 2005. *The Healing Power of the Human Voice*. Rochester, VT: Healing Arts Press.

George, Mike. 2003. *Learn to Find Inner Peace*. London: Duncan Baird Publishers Ltd.

Lyle, Lesley. 2014. *Laugh Your Way to Happiness*. Oxford: Watkins Publishing Limited.

McKeown, Patrick. 2010. *Anxiety Free*. Moycullen, Co Galway: Patrick McKeown.net.

Rakhimov, Artour. 2014. *Normal Breathing: The Key to Vital Health*. CreateSpace Independent Publishing Forum.

Rodenburg, Patsy. 2007. *Presence*. London: Penguin Books.

Schneider, Meir. 2012. *Vision for Life: Ten Steps to Natural Eyesight Improvement*. Berkeley, CA: North Atlantic Books.

Tolle, Eckhart. 2006. *A New Earth*. London: Penguin Books.

13. Energy and fatigue

The importance of rest and sleep

> **❝Diminished energy contributes to fatigue, depression, and low vitality.❞**
>
> *Sondra Barrett*

From Sondra Barrett, 2013, *Secrets of Your Cells.* Reprinted with permission.

Aims of chapter

- To learn more about the importance of sleep and rest.
- To learn about the effects of fatigue on your clients, and therefore the outcomes of therapy.
- To learn how to manage our personal energy and live with fatigue (low energy).

Importance of rest and sleep

Everybody needs adequate rest and sleep in order to function effectively. This is because through rest and sleep we restore, regenerate and rejuvenate our bodies and minds. Sleep is particularly important as that is when our bodies heal best, we recover from the day's activities, and we recharge ourselves for the next day.

Without sufficient rest we will experience decreased alertness and a dampened immune system, making us more susceptible to illnesses, impaired memory and cognitive ability, longer healing times, and muscles that don't function as well – even those that open our eyes and keep them open. Fatigue also makes focusing our eyes extremely difficult; in fact, focusing on and attending to anything, such as when a client is listening to you, will be very difficult. With reduced consciousness, our limited mind is even more limited – we experience reduced mental agility and clarity. Any capacity to attend is drawn towards the feelings of fatigue – heavy eyes, weary muscles, unclear thinking, foggy head and tension in the head. It is like having pain – it is difficult to focus on anything else. The symptoms and their corresponding "stories" (see below) shout louder than anything else and consequently they consume our attention – making it even harder to process other things going on around us. Meeting any challenges will be more testing, and "While the body can dig into its reserves for a few days, [a] prolonged time of inadequate sleep is virtually guaranteed to reduce your effectiveness at anything you attempt to do" (Stack, 2008). In short, your client will be working at a significant disadvantage if they are tired; the fatigue will be disabling them and preventing you from working together as effectively as you would otherwise be able to.

It is impossible to function at our best when tired/sleep-deprived.

Everything seems worse when we are tired. Emotions can feel more overwhelming. We are more likely to resort to old patterns of behaviours and responses – the well-worn grooves (neural circuitry). We react more instead of choosing how to respond. Bearing this in mind, it is no wonder that sleep deprivation has been used as a form of torture.

Energy and its benefits for clients

Energy is our potential for doing things. It "is a measure of how strong, invigorated, or up to a task you may feel at any moment" (Stack, 2008). Fatigue is low energy. Feeling energised is the opposite of feeling fatigued. When you have energy you have increased capacity to work towards your goals and increased chances of achieving them. When you are tired you are incapacitated. You can't expect a client to fully engage if tired. Therefore, conserving and improving energy levels need to be priorities for your client where possible.

Causes of fatigue

There are many possible causes of fatigue which can result in temporary symptoms, but it can also be a chronic problem. Likely physical causes include hunger/low blood sugar, nutritional deficiencies/poor diet ("You build one billion cells a day and you get the material to build those cells from your diet . . . so anything that is introduced to your diet literally becomes you" (Bergman, 2014) – crisps and chocolate bars then are not going to be the best foods to build you up), food sensitivities – most often caused by wheat, dairy, eggs and sugar, dehydration, medical conditions (encourage your client to check with their GP if this is a possibility that has not been already been investigated), excessive EMF (electromagnetic fields) exposure and insomnia due to use of certain drugs or pain (which can also make it more difficult to relax). Additionally stroke survivors often experience increased fatigue following a recent event (this improves over time). Furthermore, because it is normal to not tune into our bodies' methods of communication, we may miss early warning signs that we need to have a break, or we may notice them but are unable to afford ourselves the time out to rest our weary selves.

However, the cause of fatigue and insomnia is often due to our negative thinking – fears, worries, anger and anxiety. But it can also be caused by a sense of ennui, a lack of curiosity or a feeling of zest for anything, which results in feeling listless, apathetic and feeling you are being dragged along by life. Then there is an imbalance in our lives – a lack of joy which helps pump the energy through our bodies.

Any thinking takes up energy, and when this stirs up significant negative emotions much more energy is consumed. According to Deepak Chopra (1987), "strong emotion results in a sense of physical weakness, inability to act, confusion, and finally exhaustion." The emotions and the resulting fatigue are all stressful experiences. Low energy is then further depleted by the consequences of stress. According to Sondra Barrett in her book *Secrets of Your Cells* (2013), stress is a "rapid mobilisation of lifesaving energy" in a "fight or flight" situation. Therefore, significant amounts of energy are suddenly used up to deal with the immediate perceived danger. Barrett also goes on to say, "When we are stressed, our cells take in less oxygen, and when that happens they can only make about one-tenth the amount of energy as when we are breathing deeply and relaxed." Stress, then can decimate our energy reserves. Long-term stress can leave us continually drained and feeling like we're going about our day wading through mud.

We may continue to ignore our bodies and the cries they are sending out to us to rest because of the expectations we have of ourselves. Perhaps because we expect ourselves to be on form 100% of the time, regardless of how much down time we have – or haven't had. Perhaps we feel at the mercy of or pulled in various directions by "external" pressures and have no control over managing the use of our energy. Perhaps it is so ingrained in us to always be active and productive, and not doing anything (active resting) is regarded as lazy. Many of us are not in the habit of connecting with our inner bodies, not expecting to experience or enjoy our physical experience or take the time to nurture our physical form.

But if we don't acknowledge and manage our energy sufficiently in the long-term, our bodies will take control and force us to rest due to an illness we no longer have the capacity to resist. Deepak Chopra (1987) writes, "Some psychologists have suggested that fatigue appears as a warning signal and that symptoms of it are self-protecting." The lack of energy stops you from being able to do things or putting yourself in situations that are not good for you. Chopra also writes that it may also be due to an unconscious desire to be "inactive, for whatever hidden reason".

Another factor to consider is the amount of exercise that is undertaken. Muscles are where our energy reserves are. "Large muscles are the primary source of energy; it may seem paradoxical, but the more you work them, the more energy you will have" (Barrett, 2013). Also, exercise provides cells with more oxygen.

On top of feeling the effects of fatigue, the negativity you then feel about being tired and any sleep issues drain you more. Consequently, fatigue can be a difficult cycle to break.

Improving energy levels: protecting and prioritising our use of personal energy

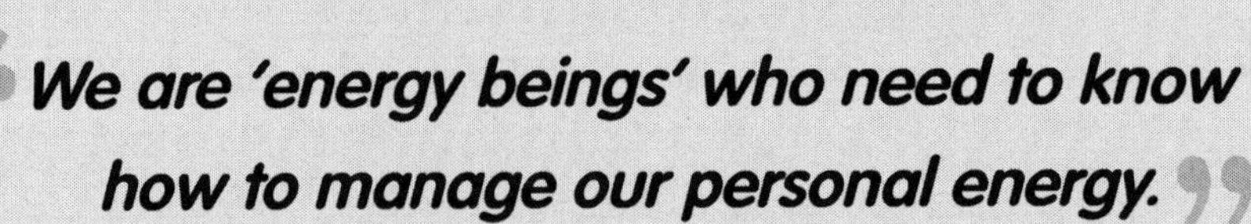

Sondra Barrett

From Sondra Barrett, 2013, *Secrets of Your Cells*. Reprinted with permission.

We have a finite amount of energy. We can think of it as a bank deposit – if you take energy out, you need to put it back in to maintain a healthy balance. It is a cycle of rest and activity that we need to honour. To work with this system we need to understand ourselves, to know how to rest and renew ourselves – to reflect on where our energy is being spent (activities etc.), and how much at a time, and be aware if there anyone or anything that is draining you (sapping you of your enthusiasm, your life force). But also learn exactly who or what sustains you, keeps you going and even gives your energy a boost! Be clear in your mind how you are going to spend your energy each day. See below for some ideas which may help a client's energy levels.

Mindfulness and fatigue

Mindfulness can help us to accept situations when there is little we can do to improve them. By observing how we really feel – how the fatigue really feels without judgement – we can surrender to the fatigue and its consequences without adding further suffering through our resistance. If you are unable to change your energy levels because of an illness or circumstances, e.g. the demands of looking after a young family (lots of demands and limited capacity), this must then be accepted as a time for quiet and for doing less than perhaps we would like ordinarily. It may mean we have to let go of attachments to being the sort of person we would wish to be, such as "fun" mum, who has so much energy for play (even after a week of work and doing all the housework), or a supportive friend who can help out when needed.

Also, be very aware of the stories which suck you in and exacerbate your suffering. They are linked to your attachments and expectations (beliefs – which are clearly not true because the reality is different). Consider how you would feel without those thoughts (affirmations or stories). Thoughts such as "I'm so tired all the time", "I'm so fed up", "poor me", "here we go", "this is not fair", or "it shouldn't happen". The cycle of self-pity is powerful – powerfully draining.

You are being forced to slow down or even stop, and right now in this moment there is little you can do but accept that. You may need to remind yourself that it has not always been like this – the voice in your head will be trying to tell you otherwise.

This is an opportunity to practise listening to your body, and get to know it better and understand what makes you tired. Is it really all the time or does it fluctuate during the day, week, or month?

When you understand yourself and the situation, the more you will have a clearer perspective. You will be less likely to put pressure on yourself as you will be more understanding of yourself and what you expect of yourself – fatigue is disabling, so give yourself a break and go easy on yourself. This is exactly what your body is asking of you – understand the fatigue if possible (cause and symptoms) and be gentle with yourself.

This is also an opportunity to practise a surrendering of the body, to remember that you are not your body – or the fatigue. You can use the visualisation and meditation below to help gain this insight. Also, saying "Fatigue is there" rather than "I am tired" can help to keep the feelings in perspective – as separate from you. This shift can make a significant difference to how you feel about the fatigue.

As thinking consumes energy, this is more incentive to practise mindfully observing your thoughts; this will naturally slow the thoughts and transform them so they are less negative. Also, as actively thinking is difficult, this can actually be positive as you can focus on the space between any thoughts which allows for fresh inspirations. Just try it – if you want to deal with a problem don't force any thoughts, just have the intention that you want to consider it, without pressure, without expectations. Watch your thoughts and allow the spaces between them – the nothingness – and see what flashes of insight just come to you.

Summary

- Fatigue makes it very difficult to carry out any tasks (which will impact on therapy) and live the life we want. It is frustrating and can be hard to accept.

- By understanding our personal energy, working with it and helping ourselves by doing things that we know will boost our energy to offset anything that depletes us and mindfully accepting fatigue when necessary, we can optimise our energy levels, learn to live with them and not reduce our energy further with negative thinking and resistance.

Activities

To aid mindfulness/acceptance

- Encourage the client to be kind and gentle to themselves – to avoid getting annoyed with themselves and to reflect on their expectations. Their arms are "tied behind their backs" when tired. They need to be patient with themselves.

- Encourage the client to stay with their feelings of fatigue. Take the time to really feel it. Where is it? Encourage them to be clear and definite in their own minds. What are they really feeling? Avoid using the usual words to describe it and just feel. It may be different to what they imagined. Observing and allowing, not resisting, will help retain the energy they have.

- Visualise to help let go of the body – imagine being transparent. Feel the inner formless self/energy, rather than the physical self.

To improve energy levels

- Encourage your client to listen to their body. If they are beginning to feel tired, they should rest if possible. Don't wait until exhaustion sets in.

- Encourage getting enough sleep.

- Encourage the client to be aware of the times of day they have more energy – work with it where possible/encourage understanding of themselves.

- Change things! If they are stuck in a rut with routines, and they are not content with their day-to-day life, add variety wherever possible – even if only in small ways.

- Be creative – doing something they love generates energy and they will find joy.

- Encourage the client to get tired in a healthy way by doing activities that are worthwhile to them, that they enjoy, and perhaps give them a sense of purpose. These activities can energise the client. Can they do more than they think? Encourage the client to consider a time, for example, that they felt very tired but then a good friend came over, and all of a sudden they felt much more energised. Could they put more effort in? Perhaps not, but it is something to consider.

- Exercise – the client can find an appropriate form that they enjoy and will therefore keep up.

- Taking a slow, mindful walk outside, alone and preferably in nature. Refresh and restore themselves with fresh air.

- Mindful stretching/yoga.

- Work on posture.

- Singing and humming – alone or in a group.

- Doing activities such as strumming a guitar or playing a piano (even if you do not know how to play), or listening to music mindfully.

- Doing all activities slowly – and mindfully if possible, e.g. brushing teeth, sitting on public transport. Doing less and expecting less of themselves.

- Affirmations – client can consider what affirmations they are currently using, e.g. "This is awful" or "I'm always tired", and change them for "I have so much energy!" or "I feel energised!" This can be very helpful in achieving mind over matter (see chapters: "The Power of the Mind" and "Affirmations"). But combine this with being aware of the needs of the body – do not try to plough on if genuinely tired, rest as needed (if possible).

- Work on breathing (see chapter: "The Breath").

- Acknowledge and express emotions and release negativity, anger (if directed at someone this is best done alone – once the anger is acknowledged the client can be more effective in dealing with the person/situation), worries and tension. Mindfully bring emotions into their awareness and allow them to change/dissipate (see chapter: "Understanding Emotions and Moods").

- Have a massage.

- Laugh whenever possible – make an effort to do this more; for example, watch comedies rather than dramas.

- Clapping. According to Lesley Lyle in her book *Laugh Your Way to Happiness* (2014), clapping stimulates acupressure points which increases energy.

- Learn some Qi Gong exercises.

- Do less – learning to say no, and allowing themselves to just "be". Just sit doing nothing but being mindfully aware of what they are experiencing within themselves and outside of themselves.

Taking the time to recharge daily is very important to be able to function effectively. Clients will benefit if they become more aware of how they are using their energy (it is precious); they can choose consciously. Also, go by what they can do when less tired – that is closer to their potential, (not by what they struggle with when tired).

To aid sleep

- If your client has difficulty falling asleep due to worries, encourage them to write down all their concerns, or write a "to do" list if they feel they have too much on their plate, prior to getting into bed.

- Increase awareness of old stories regarding sleep, e.g. "I can never fall asleep easily" (self-fulfilling prophecy) and let them go. Clients can change their affirmations when they are aware of them.

- Meditate/listen to a guided meditation (see chapter: "Meditation"). The word "meditation" may put some people off as it may seem like too big a thing, too arduous to try when they are so tired. Try not using the word "meditation", and instead call it relaxation.

- Getting out of the mind and into the body. Repeating silently "body, body, body" over and over whilst increasing awareness/attention on the body will help to calm the body and mind.

- Repeat silently "calm" – this does help to calm you, due to the meaning of the word but also the sounds.

- Other affirmations, e.g. repeat silently "slow", or "I am being guided to a long, sweet, restful sleep."

- Progressive relaxation (see chapter: "Stress versus Relaxation").

- Practice mindfulness of breath (see chapter: "The Breath").

- Encourage your client to consider their bedtime routine – do they use screens (such as watching the late news) or work in bed? Encourage doing things that help them to relax in the last half an hour before bed, e.g. listen to relaxing music, have a chamomile tea, use lavender oil in a diffuser or meditate.

- Warn against fighting sleepless nights – your client needs to accept when they happen. They need to be kind and gentle to themselves and allow sleep to happen in its own time – accept you can't always choose the moment.

- If your client can't sleep for an extended period, such as an hour, suggest they get up and repeat the bedtime routine then try again later.

- Try essential oils, e.g. lavender or Bach Rescue Remedy, to aid sleep. (Ensure they research how to use essential oils and which ones would suit them as they are potent; therefore care needs to be taken when using them).

- Sleeping grounded. Research has shown that sleeping with a sheet which you plug in to mimic the energy you receive when your skin is in contact with the Earth – grass, gravel, dirt, sand or concrete, is beneficial for many things including sleep.

References

Barrett, Sondra. 2013. *Secrets of Your Cells*. Boulder, CO: Sounds True Inc.

Bergman, John. 2014. *Depression: The Mechanical Cause*. CreateSpace Independent Publishing Platform.

Chopra, Deepak. 1987. *Creating Health:* Boston, MA: Houghton Mifflin.

Lyle, Lesley. 2014. *Laugh Your Way to Happiness*. Oxford: Watkins Publishing Limited.

Stack, Laura. 2008. *The Exhaustion Cure*. New York, NY: Broadway Books.

14. Self-love and self-compassion

From Anita Moorjani, 2012, *Dying to Be Me*. Reprinted with permission.

Aims

- To reflect on the lack of self-love that is pervasive in our society.

- To understand the negative impact on therapy of a client's lack of self-love and compassion for themselves.

- To understand the benefits of taking the time to consciously love ourselves more.

Lack of self-love is normal for us

True, authentic, constant, unconditional self-love is not commonplace in our society. Most people have no awareness of this and how detrimental this is for us all, as individuals and as a society. Very little attention of any real significance is focused on encouraging deep unconditional self-love as we grow up, in fact in many cases the opposite is true. As children, doing and achieving are where our attention has been focused, doing things and studying subjects that adults have decided are more worthwhile (e.g. maths instead of the arts) to the depths and standards set by them. Just being happy within ourselves, and being allowed to learn what our likes and dislikes are and explore our talents freely and without fear in our own time at our own readiness, is not an option in our society. In short, to be free to be ourselves. We are given praise (interpreted as love by children) for attainment of results, even if it is simply finishing all the roast potatoes on your plate (which you may love anyway). Now you do it for the adult, no longer for yourself. We thus lose touch with our inner selves, knowing how to please ourselves and how good and satisfying that feels – we lose our close connections to the delights of our senses and the joy of focusing on the moment as it is. We instead get more caught up in others' reactions rather than the reality of the moment. In fact, it may be inferred to us that it is selfish to do this. Instead we jump through the required hoops and we press the correct buttons in the adults around us and receive the reaction (big expression of love) that we have come to crave. But to receive this we must get good grades, jump high enough, beat others in competitions and be better than other people. At the same time, we have also been discouraged from becoming too full of ourselves, too self-important. "Unfortunately, a consequence of not wanting to be 'too big for your boots' can be a lifetime of playing small and apologetic, which gives birth to a sense of [being] not enough and also interferes with achievement" (Hamilton, 2015). We have received mixed messages, therefore it is impossible to love ourselves whatever we do – we can't win! Ultimately our sense of positive self-worth is fragile – based on others' opinions and readily taken away by them.

> We have not been taught to discover what makes us happy, how to enjoy and value ourselves or to take time to value just being, instead of always doing and performing.

We look for love outside ourselves

This continues into adulthood. All too often our attention is on getting love from others – a partner, family and friends. In our society we place our attention on this love that comes to us, which we don't always have control of (depending on others' moods and whims) and is usually conditional. We try to please others to attain and maintain these feelings of goodwill that are extended to us from those around us, and a lot of effort – consciously or unconsciously – is put into doing this. We value their love, and it makes us feel good about ourselves.

However, the most important person to love me – is me

When we love ourselves we feel more in control; we are more independent and capable. We don't rely on others for love and support and we can give ourselves plenty of what we need – "You do not expect the world or anyone else to reward you for being good" (Rowe, 2003). This feeds our self-confidence, allows us to be more compassionate with ourselves, frees our creativity – allows us to give things a try without worrying about our failure and our inability to react well to that. It allows us to explore our potential without harsh judgements to hold us back. It sets us free.

> Self-love is not selfish or narcissistic. It is simply wishing yourself well, just as you would for just about anyone else.

Without making a conscious effort to love, encourage and support ourselves, the fears we have picked up in childhood persist. We will be more resistant "to having a go" at something different or that looks like it might be a bit tricky, particularly in front of others (as their opinion of us matters far more and is more valid than ours is). We will be quick to criticise and attack ourselves for the slightest wrong-doing or perceived failure. We will likely taunt ourselves with such memories repeatedly (but completely unnecessarily). In short, we self-flagellate. We may not even be aware of the extent to which we are doing it; we may feel that we feel ok about ourselves. But the chances are that we could all benefit from actively loving ourselves more.

Consciously working on self-love offsets the negativity we are subjected to by the harsh voice in our head and helps to quiet it [see chapter: *"Mindfulness and the Voice in Our Head"*].

"If you make friends with yourself you will never be alone."

– attributed to Maxwell Maltz

Mindfulness and self-love and self-compassion

Through developing mindfulness you take the pressure off yourself by observing yourself without judgment, demands or criticism, from a peaceful, comfortable place which provides space for you to be, where there is no judgement, no pressure. You consciously observe and allow and accommodate everything you say or do, or think or feel. You are the observer, not the judge. As you observe and grow in awareness so will your compassion for yourself as you increasingly understand yourself and the situation you are in.

Mindfulness practice increases tolerance, and acceptance of anything you are aware of – including any negative feelings you have towards yourself – allows them to be and then to change without effort. Therefore you don't need to fear feeling worse as you become aware of your feelings towards yourself – how hard you have been on yourself. As the Dalai Lama writes in *The Art of Happiness* (1999), "The only factor that can give you refuge from the destructive effects of anger and hatred is your practice of tolerance and patience." This is what mindfulness offers.

Encouraging self-love with clients

When we support a loved one trying at something important to them, for example at a football match, how do we show that support and encouragement? Often loudly and enthusiastically! A coach would encourage their team with a pep talk before the game. But does anyone give themselves pep talks or such wholehearted support? "Yay, come on me!" "I can do it!" "Keep going!" "Nearly there!"

As you have likely witnessed first-hand in therapy sessions, clients are often quick to do the exact opposite and can get very annoyed with themselves. So much so that it can be difficult to move them on from self-berating to have another go. Clients disable themselves, hold themselves back in therapy and stop themselves achieving their true potential due to this kind of harsh treatment of themselves. It consumes therapy time, clients' energy and much of their attention. When such negative energy is generated by and directed at the client, it creates more tension inside the client and does not result in a productive therapy session.

Just increasing clients' awareness of how they treat themselves and their high expectations of themselves compared to how they would treat others in their situation can help to curb such negative behaviours.

The more clients are aware of their own treatment towards themselves, the less they are likely to do it as they will see it is not helpful; in fact it is detrimental to their progress in therapy sessions.

> **" You have the freedom to think anything you want [about yourself]. So why would you want to belittle yourself? "**
>
> *Louise L. Hay*

From Louise Hay, 2004, *I Can Do It*. Reprinted with permission.

Summary

- We have learnt during our childhood to be harsh to ourselves and to withhold love, support and compassion.

- This imbalance of warmth and support versus unforgiving judgements creates fear and causes clients to hold back from trying and engaging as much as they could in therapy sessions.

- Increasing clients' awareness of this can help them participate fully in therapy.

Activities

- Remind client as often as necessary to be kind and gentle to themselves.

- *Reflection* – reflect with the client on the sort of things they would be saying to a friend who was in their situation. What would they expect of them?

- *Reflection* – talk through with the client how to support themselves with their thoughts by making a note of any critical thoughts they have about themselves and changing it to a compassionate one.

For example:

"I am useless; I can't do this task."

Can become: "I am improving with each practice. As I stop focusing on how much I can't do it, it is easier for me to put all my effort into the task and see what I can really do."

If the client does this repeatedly whenever they are aware of a critical thought, they will rewire the brain so that compassion rather than harsh criticism is the norm (see chapter: "Affirmations").

- *Imagery* – encourage the client to imagine stepping outside themselves, standing next to themselves and offering positive encouragement/support. Or even imagine a future or past self, hugging them and offering reassurance. They can do this regularly. They can then know that they are themselves the source of their inner strength and courage and know they can always rely on it.

- Loving-kindness meditation

You will probably want to discuss what will happen in this meditation and the purpose of it prior to using it with a client. Some clients may not be open to this meditation or may not be ready for it. See how they respond to you when you first discuss self-love and try other meditations first.

"Make yourself comfortable. Sit back against the chair, feet on the floor. Imagine there is a string attached to the top of your head pulling your head upwards, and in turn straightening your spine. Let your shoulders hang down and rest your hands comfortably in your lap.

"Focus on your breath. Just observe it. Let your breath come and go; there is no need to control it.

"All your muscles are relaxing more and more. Relaxation is spreading throughout your body from your scalp and forehead, cheeks, tongue. Your eyeballs soften. Your neck, shoulders, arms, all the way past your elbows to your wrists, hands and fingers. Your chest and back, your stomach, your legs all the way down past your knees to your ankles, your feet and toes. You are becoming more and more relaxed. More and more calm. If your mind wanders just gently bring your awareness back to your body.

"Now picture yourself in your mind's eye. See yourself in a place you love to be, it can be real or imaginary. See yourself as another good friend. See yourself as happy and enjoying yourself. Approach yourself as you would to greet a friend – perhaps hug or touch your hand.

"Observe yourself. Wish yourself well. Wish yourself peace. Wish yourself happiness. Be filled with loving-kindness for yourself; feel the warmth towards yourself. Smile at yourself. Let any hardness towards yourself melt away. Be filled with compassion and understanding for yourself. You are doing your best. All you need of yourself and for yourself is patience and kindness, gentleness, and sincere and loving care. You can allow yourself all the time you need. You can allow yourself to make mistakes. It happens, because you are human. Because you are human you can cope with this because you feel the love and warmth being directed through you and to you. Nothing else matters. You feel the loving-kindness and the peace within – this is constant. Everything else can change but that inner core of love and peace is always there, if you just take the time to find it. There is nothing more important. You can always have a sense of well-being, of peace.

"Now think of a loved one. See them in this same place that you love, with you. Wish them well. Wish them peace. Wish them happiness. May they be filled with loving-kindness; feel the warmth you have for them. Smile at them. May they feel the ever-present loving-kindness and peace within. May they always have a sense of well-being, of peace.

"Now think of a neutral person. Someone you may see at the shops sometimes or on the bus. See them in this same place that you love, with you and your loved one. Wish them well. Wish them peace. Wish them happiness. May they be filled with loving-kindness; feel the warmth you have for them. Smile at them. May they feel the ever-present loving-kindness and peace within. May they always have a sense of well-being, of peace.

"Now think of a difficult person. See them in this same place that you love, with you, your loved one and the neutral person. Wish them well. Wish them peace. Wish them happiness. May they be filled with loving-kindness; feel the warmth you have for them. Smile at them. May they feel the ever-present loving-kindness and peace within. May they always have a sense of well-being, of peace.

"Feel the loving-kindness flow through you to all these people. Now extend this to everyone, to people you know and people you don't know. Enjoy feeling kindly and friendly to everyone. Send these feelings of well-being and happiness out and they will be returned to you.

"Enjoy the shared happiness, kindness, compassion and peace for a few moments.

"When you are ready, start to be aware of the chair beneath you, the floor. Hear the sounds in the room and any coming from outside the room. Stretch or move your arms and hands, your legs and feet. When you are ready open your eyes."

References

Hamilton, David R. 2015. *I Heart Me*. London: Hay House UK Ltd.

Hay, Louise L. 2004. *I Can Do It*. Carlsbad, CA: Hay House Inc.

HH Dalai Lama and Cutler, Howard C. 1999. *The Art of Happiness*. New York: Penguin.

Moorjani, Anita. 2012. *Dying to Be Me*. Carlsbad, CA: Hay House Inc.

Rowe, Dorothy. 2003. *Depression*. Hove, East Sussex: Routledge.

15. Understanding emotions and moods

Emotions and moods come, and they go.

Aims

- To help reduce clients' distress if absorbed by negative moods.

- For the client to learn to see moods for what they really are in order to release themselves from them and allow them to pass, thereby allowing the client to move on and refocus their attention to therapy tasks.

Emotions and moods

An emotion, according to Daniel Goleman (1996), refers "to a feeling and its distinctive thoughts, psychological and biological states, and range of propensities to act". There are many types of emotions, and they are short-lived, whereas "A 'mood' refers to the general tone of emotion across a period of time" (Harris, 2007). Moods are less intense, and are generally considered either positive or negative. According to the Dalai Lama (1999), "negative mental states are not an intrinsic part of our minds; they are transient obstacles that obstruct the expression of our natural state of joy and happiness."

What society teaches us about emotions and moods

Intense outbursts of emotions are typically discouraged in our society, and we shy away from dealing with negative moods in others. Society is intolerant of and lacks the capabilities to manage emotions in ourselves and in others because we have not experienced constructive modelling in childhood of how to deal with them effectively.

We are taught to suppress or avoid strong, negative feelings such as anger – perhaps we are met with more anger and told firmly to "stop it", or offered sweets to put an end to the situation the adults around us do not like to deal with, when what was really needed was love and understanding to get through the strong and scary feelings, and reassurance that they will pass. Instead we learn having and certainly expressing what is going on inside us is not acceptable if strong and particularly if "unpleasant", and so we may be fearful of doing so. If we do, we make ourselves vulnerable to other people's strong reactions: it's safer not to reveal our true emotions, but to behave in the way society expects of us. Consequently we learn to disconnect from how we feel – emotionally and physically. We disconnect from ourselves. The emotions continue but instead of flowing freely they build up inside of us, adding to stress levels and diverting our attention from dealing with situations effectually.

Emotions and moods come and go

Very often emotions and moods are referred to like the weather, and we are the sky. Therefore, we are not the clouds or the wind or the storms; we are the calm waiting behind the weather. The weather is always changing, but we can allow it to pass. This is a useful analogy to see emotions and moods for what they really are (not us), which can help release us from them and allow them to do what moods do – come and go, even though they may be hard to bear at the time. Jill Bolte Taylor (2009) adds, "Although there are certain limbic system (emotional) programs that can be triggered automatically, it takes less than 90 seconds for one of these programs to be triggered, surge through our body, and then be completely flushed out of our blood stream."

When we know this, it can change our relationship with our moods and emotions, "We learn to be with the whole passing show. As we become more accepting, a certain lightness develops about it all" (Goldstein, 2011).

What influences our emotions and moods

Our emotions and moods are a result of how we interpret situations. As David Burns (1999) writes, "It is an obvious neurological fact that before you can experience any event, you must process it with your mind and give it meaning. You must *understand* what is happening to you before you can *feel* it." Some events, such as the death of a loved one, are never going to leave us feeling good and happy. Bereavement is a normal process we have to go through. But events can trigger different reactions in different people depending on how we have perceived and interpreted it. Mood disorders arise when thoughts and feelings become pathological, as in the case of "immobilizing depression, over-whelming anxiety, raging anger, manic agitation" (Goleman, 1996).

Thoughts and feelings are additions to our mind – like clouds are additions to the sky.

Negative emotions and moods are therefore reactions – reactions can be seen as additions in our mind (extra layers of thoughts, feelings and stories), which cover up "our natural state of well-being and inner peace, the source of true happiness" (Tolle,

2006). Anthony De Mello (1990) agrees that "Every time you are unhappy, you have added something to reality. . . . You have added . . . a negative reaction in you. Reality provides the stimulus, you provide the reaction." De Mello states this is due to having illusions, expectations and attachments.

Burns (1999) also writes that negative thoughts are automatic thoughts. These automatic thoughts are due to our subconscious programming. As we know, our subconscious is the main force that controls our lives and "The actions of the subconscious mind are reflexive in nature" (Lipton, 2015), therefore our programming mostly dictates how we are going to perceive and react to situations. Our buttons that can be readily pushed and trigger a mood are already wired into us, and we are often not aware of these patterns of behaviour. With little awareness of how moods can begin it is difficult to then see situations differently and respond differently.

Moods can also be influenced and exacerbated by various other factors. We may even be at the mercy of forces we are unaware of; for example, eating certain foods, hunger, low blood sugar, fatigue and pain, excessive exposure to electromagnetic fields, addiction to mobile devices such as smart phones and even pre- and perinatal influences can affect moods. These are additional elements that can make us feel out of control, which only serve to create fear around moods and emotions and intensify experiences of negative moods.

As we experience our situations and emotions we also create stories in our minds about them based on our beliefs. These stories then get played on a loop; they become hard-wired, fuel the intensity of our feelings and prolong the mood. These stories will usually be very negative and focus on how we are lacking – personally, materially and in our life situation. "It shouldn't be like this", "If only . . .", "I don't deserve . . ." – these thoughts represent the gist of what we tell ourselves. This is all fighting and resisting our circumstances and our feelings. But when you fight something you give it power and anchor it in place; resistance then encourages these thoughts and moods to dominate your life.

> **_Feeling out of balance – when things feel worse and worse._**
>
> Chris Williams

From Chris Williams, 2008, *Overcoming Depression and Low Mood*, p. 23.
Reprinted with permission.

Generally we are able to cope with the demands in our lives and we feel we can manage problems that arise. But with all these strong influences at play within us, it is no wonder we commonly feel out of balance at times as life presents challenging issues, and especially at times when they are heaped one on top of the other with no hope of things improving. This is when low moods can set in.

Moods influence thoughts: the cycle

Thoughts drive moods, but moods also drive thoughts. "In practice, this means that even a few fleeting moments of sadness can end up feeding off themselves to create more unhappy thoughts by colouring how you see and interpret the world" (Williams and Penman, 2011). Goleman (1996) also notes,

> People have what amounts to a set of bad-mood thoughts that come to mind more readily when they are feeling down. People who get depressed easily tend to create very strong networks of association between these thoughts, so that it is harder to suppress them once some kind of bad mood is evoked.

It is easy to see how we can end up in a cycle of low mood which can spiral.

On top of all this if you have been experiencing challenging circumstances or surrounded by difficult and negative people (mood vampires – we pick up on others' energy) for an extended period of time you can get out of the habit of smiling and experiencing joy. Happy muscles (e.g. those used for smiling) atrophy along with the associated neural networks in the brain. Low-energy moods get stuck and further entrenched.

When moods persist

If low or challenging moods persist, you will need to refer the client to the relevant services available or encourage them to see their GP for further help.

Managing emotions and moods: mindfulness techniques

Emotions and moods in perspective

When in the grips of a strong mood it can feel like we are possessed, as if we are in the middle of the storm and we can't escape it. But by learning to change perspective on our feelings we can separate ourselves from them. The moods are *in us, not out there* in the external reality, but they are not us. As Anthony De Mello (1990) writes,

> The reason you suffer from your [moods] is that you identify with them. You say, "I'm depressed." But that is false. You are not depressed . . . you might say "I am experiencing a depression right now". But . . . you are not your depression. [This] . . . is but a strange kind of trick of the mind, a strange kind of illusion.

Feelings can also be likened to noise – noise is just noise, something that is there that you are experiencing. You don't need to fear feelings even though they are unpleasant. Mark Williams and Danny Penman call it "fusing" when we think our feelings are us – we feel that we and our mood are one and the same thing. Making this shift in our thinking can make a big difference to how we manage moods.

Step outside the mood – you are not your emotions and moods.

Observe without judgement

When we are attempting to be mindful of our feelings, we are focusing on observing all emotions and moods as a detached onlooker, like a third person, with an attitude of openness and curiosity. You just watch moods come and go. You will also need to watch your thoughts at the same time, observe how they are judging your feelings. There is no need to label a mood as happy or sad – what does that really mean right now? Connect with the sensations, not the words which are barriers; this involves a moment-by-moment contact with reality. Labels are part of the stories and unnecessarily add to the strength of feelings. The key is to allow them all, make space for them all. Bolte Taylor (2009) describes the process in this way,

> The healthiest way I know how to move through an emotion effectively is to surrender completely to that emotion when its loop of physiology comes over me. I simply resign to the loop and let it run its course for 90 seconds.

It may be particularly difficult and painful initially, we may even be afraid to try – we may fear the feelings and imagine them to be worse than they are,

> the overwhelming temptation is to withdraw [recoil from the feelings] . . . [you are fearful of your strong emotions] . . . fear is your secret that knee-jerks you out of . . . [your mindful awareness], away from thoughts and feelings you cannot meet.
>
> (Rodenburg, 2007)

However, in mindfulness practice it is important to turn towards your feelings and stay with them, knowing that this will all pass as nothing can stay the same – as long as you stay conscious of them, otherwise "When you are not in your body . . . an emotion can survive inside you for days or weeks . . . [or] years, feed on your energy, lead to physical illness, and make your life miserable" (Tolle, 2005). As Sophie Sabbage (2015) writes, "If you don't have your feelings, then your feelings will have you."

Observing and staying with thoughts and feelings can stop the downward spiral of low moods. "You can stop the spiral from feeding off itself and triggering the next cycle of negative thoughts. You can stop the cascade of destructive emotions" (Williams and Penman, 2011). You stop it by watching what is happening whilst knowing they are just thoughts and feelings and not real – rather they are "propaganda", as Williams and Penman refer to them.

Acceptance and non-resistance

As discussed earlier, fighting feelings strengthens them so we need to completely surrender to them and allow them their time whilst being fully aware of them.

> You don't do a thing to make it go away; you are perfectly willing to go on with your life while it passes through you and disappears. . . . And you're willing to let this cloud come in, because the more you fight it, the more power you give it. You're willing to observe it as it passes by.
>
> (De Mello, 1990)

There is no way round them; you have to go through them to move on to a calm state.

Claire Weekes (1995) discusses true acceptance to be able to move on from feelings – she describes it as the stage where it no longer matters whether a feeling is there or not, you accept that it may – or may not – be there for some time, you will allow it to be.

As you do this you still have moods, but they pass more quickly. Emotions and moods demand time, attention and tolerance; if you give them what they require there will be less additional pain. As Bernhard (2011) writes "I took a deep breath and began the weather practice, remembering that thoughts and moods blow all over the place and that if I just waited, these particular ones would blow on through. And they did."

Understanding

Through mindfulness practice we are able to gain insights and understanding into the nature of our feelings, to see through them and where they are really coming from. We can see that "the only power our thoughts have is the power we give them . . . we can learn to be mindful of them and not be carried away by the meanderings of the mind" (Goldstein, 2011). You are then no longer seeing things through your filters, living with illusions and buffeted by the storms within you. As you understand the moods they will happen less intensely and less frequently. But either way it won't be so important what happens because you will feel more able to live with the moods and emotions. You may even see them as guides that lead you to positive changes in your life.

Managing emotions and moods: breaking the cycle by changing thoughts and behaviours

Thoughts

> **❝I know it is possible to create new feelings by focusing on better things.❞**
>
> Bronnie Ware

From Bronnie Ware, 2012, *The Top Five Regrets of the Dying*. Reprinted with permission.

Changing the way we think and behave is the essence of cognitive behavioural therapy (CBT). According to David D. Burns, MD (*Feeling Good*), we have an amazing ability to cling to distorted beliefs and see them as facts, which in turn colours our mood. Our beliefs are based on inaccurate thinking and a filtered reality, one in which we fixate on certain (negative) details, completely ignoring other (more positive) details, which is a bad habit we develop.

We can get into better habits of questioning thoughts and feelings and develop flexibility of thought to take on new perspectives to see the bigger picture. Then we can accommodate the issues and feelings and we don't focus on the one small part of our reality which is unhelpful and unhealthy. It can also be helpful to adopt the attitude of not knowing when it comes to our thoughts – they may be right but they may be wrong, so that you don't put so much weight on them. Thoughts come and go so quickly, as do opinions and judgements, when we remember that it is easier to hold them more lightly. We can even question how we would feel without them. So what is worse – reality or the thought about it?

Behaviour

Emotions can impact on our behaviour but they do not have to control it, so we can behave differently to how we feel. However, since behaviours influence our thinking and moods, we can change them to improve overall mood.

If low moods are occurring often, you need to consider if your life is balanced – are you enjoying enough pleasures in life to balance out the challenging times? Making time to do things you enjoy is a sign of good self-esteem and self-love. It is also an acknowledgement of being human and needing to tend to you sometimes to restore and reenergise yourself and to avoid getting exhausted and burning out. You are simply looking after yourself as you *need* to. If you are kind and compassionate to yourself, this will mean saying "no" to requests at times.

> Gradually start to make changes – change habits and thinking, then you will gradually start to see a shift in mood.

Doing things that release emotions and tension is helpful, including crying and laughing. Meditation, including mindfulness meditation, can also be extremely helpful and setting and working towards achievable goals can lift moods.

Helping others can take our minds off ourselves. It can be a reminder to be grateful for what we do have, even if it does not seem like much compared to some other people.

Be guided by moods – if you feel tired/not in a "good" mood/fed up, then simply listen, feel, accept, go with it – what are the moods telling you? Delay activities and interactions if necessary.

Moods can be improved – you can work at it; they come down to a matter of perspective. "How do I be happy? . . . You allow yourself to be. . . . Allow yourself and choose to be" (Ware, 2012). It may sound too simplistic, but changing your habits can change your life. Honour low moods when they occur but also cultivate happiness.

Moods and therapy

It is important to take into consideration how a client is feeling – their emotions and moods can be barriers to therapy. You will have to be aware of them and gently work around them as you are able. You can try to broach the subject with the client and see if they are willing to open up at all without pushing them. Also remember moods can swing in moments; a mood can be triggered by something you say or do which they have associated with something negative. It may not be personal or your fault, but you will need to be sensitive to their feelings, and plans for the session may need to be adapted accordingly. It may mean taking time out for a meditation or talking about their concerns, or even abandoning the session if necessary. It is something you will have to gauge with the client on a moment-by-moment basis.

Summary

- We all experience moods all of the time, but sometimes they can be strong and even overwhelming.

- A client's mood can affect one therapy session or all of them.

- With a clearer understanding of what moods are, mindfully observing and allowing them time and space, and accepting them and/or altering thoughts and behaviours, they can improve and become less of an issue and impact less on therapy.

Activities

- Discuss the above – what moods and emotions are and how they are part of a cycle which includes their thinking and behaviours. Discuss mindfulness techniques which can allow them to accept low moods and strong emotions so they don't have to fear them and allow them to pass through more quickly.

- Guided meditation:

"Make yourself comfortable. Sit back against the chair, feet on the floor. Imagine there is a string attached to the top of your head pulling your head upwards, and in turn straightening your spine. Let your shoulders hang down and rest your hands comfortably in your lap. Focus on your breath. Just observe it. Let your breath come and go; there is no need to control it. All your muscles are relaxing more and more.

"Now become aware of how you are feeling. Focus on all parts of your body – what do you notice? You may notice tension in certain places. It doesn't matter. Don't try to resist anything you notice, just observe it and allow it to be, and it will sort itself out. Keep scanning your body in this way. Notice any changes. Changes are fine. Be curious about the sensations – what is there? Avoid labelling any feeling; what are you actually feeling? Be open to everything you feel. Are they what you thought they were? Notice any thoughts or emotions now. What is your overall mood feeling like? Connect with how it feels. Remember to avoid naming anything you notice. It may not feel pleasant, but try to stay with it. By giving your feelings attention they can naturally disperse and pass on through when they are ready. Fighting them will only hold them in place and prevent them moving on.

"Continue to watch, observe and allow all your feelings for a few moments.

"When you are ready start to become aware of the chair beneath you, and the floor beneath your feet. Hear the sounds in the room and any coming from outside the room. Stretch or move your arms and hands, your legs and feet. When you are ready, open your eyes."

- Explore what activities they enjoy doing. Are they making time for them to balance out their lives?

- See other activities to relieve stress (see chapters: "Stress versus Relaxation", "The Body, Posture and Movement" and "The Breath").

References

Bernhard, Toni. 2011. Sickness Is Like the Weather. In Barry Boyce (ed.), *The Mindfulness Revolution*. Boston, MA: Shambhala Publications Inc., pp. 149–152.

Burns, David D. 1999. *Feeling Good*. New York, NY: Harper.

De Mello, Anthony. 1990. *Awareness*. Grand Rapids, MI: Fount Paperbacks.

Goldstein, Joseph. 2011. Here, Now, Aware. In Barry Boyce (ed.), *The Mindfulness Revolution*. Boston, MA: Shambhala Publications Inc., pp. 21–27.

Goleman, Daniel. 1996. *Emotional Intelligence*. London: Bloomsbury Publishing Plc.

Harris, Russ. 2007. *The Happiness Trap*. London: Robinson Publishing Ltd.

HH Dalai Lama and Cutler, Howard C. 1999. *The Art of Happiness*. New York: Penguin.

Lipton, Bruce H. PhD. 2015. *The Biology of Belief 10th Anniversary Edition*. London: Hay House Inc.

Rodenburg, Patsy. 2007. *Presence*. London: Penguin Books.

Sabbage, Sophie. 2015. *The Cancer Whisperer*. London: Coronet.

Taylor, Jill Bolte. 2009. *My Stroke of Insight*. London: Hodder & Stoughton.

Tolle, Eckhart. 2005. *The Power of Now*. London: Hodder and Stoughton.

Tolle, Eckhart. 2006. *A New Earth*. London: Penguin Books.

Ware, Bronnie. 2012. *The Top Five Regrets of the Dying*. Carlsbad, CA: Hay House Inc.

Weekes, Claire. 1995. *Self-Help for Your Nerves*. London: Thorsons.

Williams, Chris. 2008. *Overcoming Depression and Low Mood*. Boca Raton, FL: CRC Press.

Williams, Mark and Penman, Danny. 2011. *Mindfulness*. London: Piatkus.

16. Motivation

From Louise Hay, 2004, *I Can Do It.* Reprinted with permission

Aims

- To understand motivation and a client's lack of it.

- To reflect on ways to increase client's motivation in order to maximise therapy outcomes.

Barriers

Innate drive

As young children we are inclined to explore ourselves and our environment with little fear. According to John Holt, an educator and educational critic, in his book *How Children Learn* (1970) young children are curious, experimental and bold and they are willing to practise and are not afraid of making mistakes – this is to fill "the gap . . . make sense out of things . . . and gain competence and control over [themselves] and . . . [their] environment . . . [they are] . . . open, receptive, and perceptive." This is why and how we learn. Self-motivation is innate.

Alfie Kohn (2005) writes, "Numerous studies have confirmed that children are naturally inclined to . . . push themselves to do things just beyond their current level." He adds that it has been clearly shown "that the idea that it is natural to do as little as possible" is completely untrue. Children have a natural drive.

Learned sense of powerlessness

Through childhood this natural tendency is eroded; we come to realise we have less and less control over ourselves and our environment as we are pushed, moulded and prevented from considering for ourselves what we want to do and learn and when and how. For some people this will be more the case than for others. This is the concept of learned helplessness (a term coined by US researcher Martin Seligman) – when we have learnt that whatever we do, we can't change our situation, e.g. that we can't spell, we can't do maths, and we can't perform well in exams or interviews. We give up; we lose the will to try because it feels pointless, but particularly if we have learnt that the consequences of trying and failing are painful, we then learn to stop trying due to fear.

If individuals have never felt they have much control over what happens to them or their ability to affect things (positive changes), their confidence will be low. It is likely that some clients will feel this to varying degrees.

The role models we had when growing up will also impact on our self-motivation in adulthood. Their perception of obstacles in their lives and their willingness to try and overcome them will influence our own attitudes.

Fear

Fear is a huge barrier to motivation for clients. Fear of humiliating themselves, fear of revealing aspects of themselves, fear of what you will think of them, fear of failure, and fear of being out of their comfort zone. Therapy can be unsettling and uncomfortable for a client and they may feel insecure. These feelings will hold them back from trying things and taking risks.

A client may find it too hard to face their full reality; they may worry that reality is even worse than their fears, and fear the possibility of not being able to change anything.

It may also be possible that a client has a subconscious wish not to participate in therapy as they have a need to remain in the "sick role", which is safer than engaging with reality.

Optimists and pessimists

Our programming in childhood together with our innate temperament will determine whether we are generally optimistic or pessimistic. Optimism, according to Daniel Goleman (1996) is

> having a strong expectation that, in general, things will turn out all right in life, despite setbacks and frustrations . . . [it] is an attitude that buffers people against falling into apathy, hopelessness, or depression in the face of tough going.

Optimists are more likely to feel self-reliant, that there is something they can do, and any setbacks are seen in perspective – they can consider things outside themselves that may have affected what happened, they don't take it all personally. They see that they are not completely to blame because they are a failure, or that the setback is a sign of some personal flaw. They are more likely to try again and give themselves opportunity to practise and improve.

If a client has learned to be helpless and without hope and if they are generally pessimistic in their outlook, they are likely to have low self-esteem and self-confidence, particularly as they have grown up in a world where what you do and achieve defines you – or at least that is what they have learnt to believe.

Habitual thinking and behaviour

Programming and innate character traits lead to patterns of thinking and behaviour. According to Joe Dispenza in his book *Breaking the Habit of Being Yourself* (2012), we get too addicted to comfortable and habitual ways of thinking, feeling and doing. It becomes our habit to be ready to do what is necessary to effect change in our lives, or to sit back and allow things to happen and possibly complain about them. We cultivate high energy levels, in a state of readiness to embrace all life situations, or remain generally flat. Or we are somewhere in-between. It may feel beyond us to change that energy and remain open to new possibilities, to explore our potential, to push boundaries and discover new aspects of ourselves. It is certainly safer to stick with how you normally do things than approach anything new. But if you always do what you've always done, you'll always get what you've always got.

Goals

> Obstacles are those frightful things you see when you take your eyes off the goal.
> *– attributed to Henry Ford*

Without discovering enough joy from experiencing and achieving through their own efforts, clients may not be in the habit of setting themselves goals and keeping them in mind as they work towards achieving them. They may be more focused on obstacles or short-term pleasures – which may be the only source of pleasure (such as eating) and impede any attempts they make towards a longer-term goal.

Mood

If mood is low at the time of therapy, a client will likely be experiencing a sense of inertia, and may feel that any effort is all too much for them, they can't be bothered, they'd rather do other things or nothing at all. They may want to take the path of least resistance; therefore they have little enthusiasm for anything that requires effort.

External factors

Motivation levels are also influenced by our life circumstances – there may be too many other pressing matters going on in their life. If a client is feeling under pressure from factors unrelated to therapy, their focus and energies will not be directed on the therapy, or at least not as fully as they could. It may reach the point where life and enthusiasm are or have been sapped out of the client by situations, environment or people they are surrounded by – or even their memories.

Our judgements

Be aware of your own judgements of clients – perhaps judging them for their lack of commitment to the therapy process and labelling them, for example, as "lazy". This can be very unhelpful. Consciously or unconsciously this may affect your treatment of a client and cause you not to support or treat them to your full ability; we may give up on them more readily as they have given up on themselves. It is more useful to try to understand the reasons for their lack of motivation, in order to be more compassionate and patient and to explore ways of overcoming the barriers.

How to improve motivation

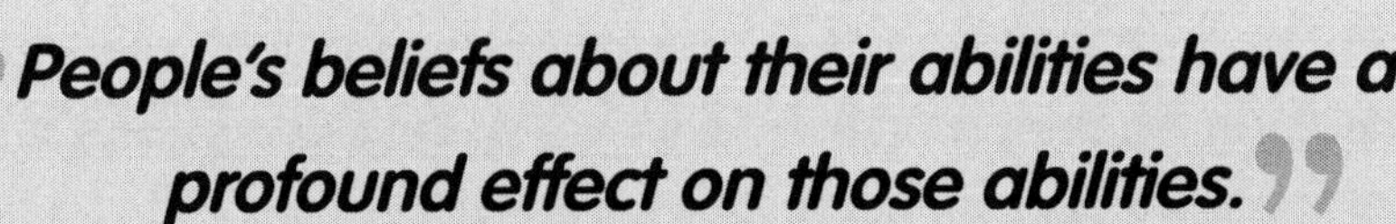

Joint planning

Work together to explore the client's situation, consider how they spend their time and energy day to day – is it getting them to where they want to be? Reflect on what they want to achieve in therapy, how they want to achieve these goals and the potential barriers to their engagement. Set timeframes can be established to review this regularly and keep the client on track.

Working on reasons to engage

If motivation is low, there needs to be sufficient impetus to change ingrained habits, ways of thinking and behaving. The potential rewards need to be a bigger pull than the security they feel from not trying. They need to see that it is important to them to try even if they are not sure what can be achieved. Trying is better than the alternative – not trying, not seeing if they could do more and achieve their goals, and never knowing the potential improvements they can make to their situation.

Talking through what they want, what goals they want to achieve, allows clients to reflect and change their focus to positive things that they could work on. You can use visualisation to make this more powerful. As long as their attention is here – on positive things – they can't simultaneously be dwelling on negative things, and it allows the draw to become stronger.

Explain your role to the client and what you can do. If you can, explain how what you do *can* help and this is why you do the job – because therapy can make a difference (you wouldn't be doing it otherwise!) – if they are willing to engage.

Working on negative self-talk and beliefs

Ask the client if they feel they are doing all they can in therapy and if not, gently talk through the reasons why they are holding back. This can be an opportunity to allow the client to see how their thoughts and beliefs are holding them back and preventing them from working towards what they want, and then to challenge those self-limiting beliefs – are they even true? Just bringing them to the surface can help the client to drop them, or at least let go of them to a degree to allow for some increased effort.

Values/purpose

Values are linked to our moral principles. They guide behaviour and extend beyond the self; it is about doing things that we perceive are important and worthwhile. Doing things based on your values can be powerful in stimulating resolve to get through something, even when things become difficult; as Russ Harris (2007) states, "Values act as motivators." Therefore they give you strength and energy, just as Viktor Frankl (2004) found when he was in the Nazi concentration camps, "Those who have a 'why' to live, can bear almost any how."

It is particularly motivating doing something that is connected to something bigger than the self, as Daniel Pink (2009) observes, "The most deeply motivated people – not to mention those who are most productive and satisfied – hitch their desires to a cause larger than themselves."

Focusing on our values and having a purpose prevents us from focusing on the self – they take us outside ourselves so we don't get caught up in personalising what we do. We can think more clearly and act more effectively because we can be more objective. It also provides sufficient interest to keep going for longer. Therefore talking through a client's values and finding purpose in the therapy process will help increase motivation.

"Determination and perseverance": affirmations

(See chapter: "Affirmations".)

Affirmations can be very useful in generating and maintaining motivation. Encourage the client to change their negative self-talk to positive affirmations. They can focus on just one or two so that it doesn't become confusing and they end up giving up on them. By repeating these statements with enthusiasm, they can improve their self-discipline and help themselves to keep going, so that a tepid response becomes a strong will to try.

Self-love

(See chapter: "Self-Love and Self-Compassion".)

Self-love is an important motivator because then you can feel that you are worth the effort to try, that you are not wasting the therapist's time, and that you can be kind and gentle to yourself if you experience setbacks when trying and allow yourself more practice. You are there for yourself and you don't expect perfection from yourself; you will love yourself whatever you do or don't do. You provide a cushion for yourself when you fall.

Self-love is the foundation to a positive upwards spiral:

The more self-love = more self-discipline = more effort = more confidence = more self-belief.

Build confidence

Avoidance is a coping strategy when people are scared of doing something, but this does nothing for confidence, as you don't give yourself a chance to build it up.

Confidence can be developed through setting small, short-term SMART goals (Specific, Measurable, Achievable, Relevant, Time-bound). When a client tries very small tasks they are beginning to face their fears, and according to Chris Williams (2008) "the very best way of tackling your fears is to face them in a planned way." Building on successes can increase self-confidence and reduce anxiety; and this can lead to increased enthusiasm and a willingness to do more. This feeling of being able to achieve in itself becomes an intrinsic motivator to engage more.

Encouragement

When people are at a low point they need help with motivation – this is when you can bring positive energy. You are in a position to encourage clients through what you say and how you say it. Enthusiasm is infectious – it is a positive energy that clients can benefit from. You can be the spark that helps clients make that first step. It may be challenging initially, and you may not see much change, but if you persevere it can benefit the client.

You can encourage (what you think is appropriate and realistic) hope, belief and optimism. But also do not dash what you perceive as a client's false hope. As Sophie Sabbage (2015) writes,

> Just as there is no such thing as grief that brings "closure", there is no such thing as "false hope". There is hope or there is none. Hope is a projection into a desired future, a feeling that something wanted or longed for could perhaps become reality. Hope doesn't make promises. It just hopes. And it is one of the most potent motivating forces I know.

A client is free to explore their potential, the unknown. Nobody really knows all outcomes; there are too many variables.

Create a safe and empowering environment

Clients need to feel involved in the planning of therapy and have an overall understanding of it in order to enhance engagement. They need to feel clear in what is going on and why, not left feeling ignorant and fearful. There needs to be balance in the therapeutic relationship, so that the client feels like an active partner in it and has a sense of control over what is happening. You can give options, for example regarding tasks, wherever possible.

Using humour can also be useful to engage clients when used appropriately. It can defuse tensions and helps them to forget themselves and their fears. If they know you are friendly and you are providing a safe environment to let down their guard, they can trust you enjoy laughing with them and not at them.

If clients see you as a guide, not a teacher-type figure, who they feel safe with and where there is mutual respect, it will ease their tensions and allow for therapy to take place more effectively. Clients will feel more secure to persevere in the face of difficulties.

Motivation and mindfulness

Mindfulness can help with motivation as it focuses us on observing with curiosity and without judgement in the here and now. You are released from the old ways of negative thinking that hold you back and are ready to actively engage. Clients will be able to focus more on listening to you or what they are doing rather than judging themselves harshly, or anticipating failure. They will then more likely experience success.

Not forcing

We need to be careful about trying to push clients too much. It is something that is dependent on the individual client at that particular moment. "Cracking the whip" can be done in humour with a client you know well, but sometimes it is not appropriate to try at all – some people, or at least in some sessions, will not be in the right place and it will be felt as extra pressure they really don't need at that time.

Also motivation levels can wax and wane and it may be a sign they need a break from therapy, particularly if it has been going on for a significant period of time. They may have reached saturation point, for now at least.

Too much motivation

The other side of the coin is when clients are already too driven and work themselves too hard. As Raj Persaud (2006) observes, "motivation has a dark side, for it is what drives us to the deepest despair in the face of disappointment." This is more commonly associated with Type A personalities who are more competitive, ambitious and impatient. They are more likely to be high achieving workaholics who relentlessly push themselves. Be aware of how much work you are giving such clients to do, how much information you are giving, and what you expect between sessions. It would be safer to err on the side of giving less if you know they are already likely to go above and beyond what you recommend. It may also be worthwhile planning when and how often they do any work independently to monitor this, and emphasise the importance of rest and sleep in the therapy process.

A client's responsibility outside and beyond therapy

Determination and perseverance ultimately come from within. Clients need to take control and responsibility for their progress in therapy. It is our job to try to engage and motivate clients but we also need to be aware when clients are not going to engage whatever we do.

Summary

- Motivation is vital for successful therapy – clients need to feel engaged and have the desire to do what is required to achieve their goals. The amount of motivation a client has will directly influence the outcomes of therapy.

- There are various reasons why a client may have low motivation; ideally, these need to be understood and taken into consideration when tailoring the therapy.

- There are also many ways to help increase a client's motivation and it is our responsibility to try to do so. However, the responsibility is ultimately the client's.

References

Bandura, Albert. 1988. quoted in *The New York Times*: www.nytimes.com/1988/04/05/science/new-scales-of-intelligence-rank-talent-for-living.html?pagewanted=all (accessed 5th June 2017).

Dispenza, Joe. 2012. *Breaking the Habit of Being Yourself*. Carlsbad, CA: Hay House Inc.

Frankl, Viktor. 2004. *Man's Search for Meaning*. London: Rider & Co.

Goleman, Daniel. 1996. *Emotional Intelligence*. London: Bloomsbury Publishing Plc.

Harris, Russ. 2007. *The Happiness Trap*. London: Robinson Publishing Ltd.

Hay, Louise L. 2004. *I Can Do It*. Carlsbad, CA: Hay House Inc.

Holt, John. 1970. *How Children Learn*. Harmondsworth: Penguin Books.

Kohn, Alfie. 2005. *Unconditional Parenting*. New York, NY: Atria Books.

Persaud, Raj. 2006. *The Motivated Mind*. London: Bantam Press.

Pink, Daniel H. 2009. *Drive*. London: Riverhead Books.

Sabbage, Sophie. 2015. *The Cancer Whisperer*. London: Coronet.

Williams, Chris. 2008. *Overcoming Depression and Low Mood*. Boca Raton, FL: CRC.

17. Attention

You are wherever your attention is.

Aims

- To learn about the importance of attention in therapy in more detail.

- To provide an opportunity to reflect on a client's ability to attend, to consider where their attention might be.

- To take into consideration possible distractions for clients and how to improve their focus in therapy.

- To help clients understand that taking control of their attention can lower stress and improve their quality of life.

Attention, concentration and focus

Quite simply attention means to take notice of something; it is the behavioural and cognitive process of selectively focusing on a particular object. In his book *The Principles of Psychology* (1981), William James elaborates on this,

> It is the taking possession of the mind, in clear and vivid form, of one out of what seem several simultaneously possible objects or trains of thought. Focalisation, concentration, of consciousness are of its essence. It implies a withdrawal from some things in order to deal effectively with others.

To clarify meanings, attention and concentration can be used interchangeably. According to Brain Tree trainers Kit Malia and Anne Brannagan (2006), there are different types of attention, including focused attention, sustained attention, and selective attention, alternating attention and divided attention. Focused attention relates to the initial and very brief (less than a second) hooking onto a stimulus (although it may not be what you want). Sustained attention refers to the ability to maintain focused attention. Selective attention is the ability to ignore distractions and remain focused, and alternating attention is the ability to change your focus between different stimuli. Divided attention is also known as multi-tasking – or consciously doing two things at the same time.

Attention can be consciously focused on something or it can be pulled by something such as a loud noise.

The importance of attention in therapy

Attention is needed to take information in; what you focus on is where you are receiving information from at any one time. Therefore it is the key to doing anything effectively, including participating in therapy.

It is a prerequisite for clients to understand and take part in conversations, remember anything, be able to cooperate in tasks, process information and reflect and draw conclusions for themselves. Therefore even though we have already talked about attention and the importance of it with regards to mindfulness, it is of such importance in itself for successful therapy outcomes that it is worth dedicating a chapter to it.

Be aware where attention is

Your reality

Attention determines what aspects of the experience available to you that you are engaging with. What you attend to makes up your reality, as Winifred Gallagher writes in her book *Rapt* (2009), "attention distils *the* universe into *your* universe." This is usually what you think is important at the time or whatever has the biggest pull, such as physical pain. We are only able to take in a small part of life – there is far too much stimuli available to attend to for us to take it all in, therefore our reality is personal and unique; it is our version of it.

Your response and experience based on your reality

What you focus on greatly determines your thinking, understanding and behaviour – your perspective, interpretation and response in a situation. For example, the difference between someone being scared of something and someone else relishing it, such as meeting new people, is the pull on their attention to different aspects (the positive or negative possibilities). Shifting your focus from worrying about what people think of you to taking an interest in them can make a huge difference to your experience in such situations.

Focusing on the negative

As you watch where your attention goes you will likely notice it tends to fixate on the negative thoughts and aspects of situations to the exclusion of all else. Negative things want to monopolise your attention. Even something very minor and trivial, such as a broken nail or something stuck in our teeth, can easily hijack our attention so that little else can make up our reality. They are just niggling things but demonstrate how a small thing can appear magnified. That is our experience of life in any given moment – what we attend to in the now.

Barriers to attending: internal and external

Attention can easily be sidetracked due to many reasons; as Russ Harris (2012) writes,

> The mind has many different ways to hijack our attention . . . it may pull us back into the past, replaying . . . painful events . . . or it may push us into the future, conjuring up all manner of fearful scenarios. It may even drag us deep into the swamp of our current problems: bogging us down in our pain and our stress and our hardship.

These are just some of the ways a client's attention can be diverted:

Worries

- The mind can readily become absorbed in worries, such as the problem they are consulting you about or everyday concerns (paying bills, taking the dog to the vet, arranging a plumber to unblock a drain etc.)

- Personal issues

- Fear of how they will be judged by you

- Feeling under pressure to "achieve" in therapy sessions

- General anxiety

- Strong emotions, e.g. as a result of their worries, which can become even more frightening and distracting in themselves

Thinking absorbs our attention. We live in a world of thought, as Russ Harris writes in *The Reality Slap* (2012),

> Let's think of our minds as master storytellers that don't care if their stories are helpful or not; their main aim is to capture our attention . . . we give it all our attention [and] . . . we generally don't lose interest. Even if we've heard this recording ten thousand times, and all it does is make us feel miserable, we still readily become fixated by it.

These fears and tensions not only divert attention from therapy but also drain clients of energy, making it even harder to attend.

Additional issues that can affect attention include

- Brain injury

- Pain

- Impaired dopamine system

- Tinnitus

- Needing the toilet

- Too much stimuli in the room, e.g. noisy environment

- Fatigue

- Poor general attention

- Low interest – clients need to be interested and motivated to attend, they may be present in body but not in mind

Mindfulness and attention

Mindfulness requires paying attention on purpose. According to Jeff Brantley (2011),

> Mindfulness benefits from the ability to concentrate attention but is not the same as concentration. It is a quality that human beings already have, but they have usually not been advised that they have it, that it is valuable, or that it can be cultivated. Mindfulness is the awareness that is not thinking but is aware of thinking, as well as each of the other ways we experience the sensory world. . . . It is cultivated by paying attention purposely, deeply and without judgment to whatever arises in the present moment, either inside or outside of us.

By developing attention then, this helps to attend mindfully – with intent to observe and understand, not judge the here and now we are in. There also needs to be awareness that you are doing it. It is a subtle difference – to be attending to something, and to be fully aware that you are attending to something. This provides some separation between your sense of self – with all its problems – and the observing part of you, which allows you to see things clearly and calmly, because at this level of awareness there is no judgement.

The power of being fully present in the now

Through moment-by-moment awareness that we are attending to thoughts, feelings and external stimuli, we connect with reality. It is through this attention and awareness that we wake up to life (which is experiencing the present moment right here, right now), that gives us the sense that "I'm alive!" to see it as it is and appreciate it – the aim of mindfulness is to do this in every moment. It also allows you to be effective where you are now. The present moment is where your power is.

By living a focused life, you are fully in the life you have.

Choose where your attention is

Observe your attention

To begin taking control of your attention you first need to mindfully observe it. Increasing consciousness of your attention, you will learn how well you can currently use it, how it is used and distracted from your intended targets, and so how you want to change it. Just being aware of how our attention shifts in this way automatically gives us more perspective and control over it. As Winifred Gallagher (2009) writes,

> by attending to . . . deliberately selected targets . . . you would have had a far better experience [than if you were] captured by whatever flotsam and jetsam happens to wash up on [your] mental shores. In short, to enjoy the kind of experience you want rather than enduring the kind that you feel stuck with, you have to take charge of your attention.

Control your attention

Our tendency is to focus on the negative, but you can choose to redirect your attention to something more positive. It may be difficult at first, but making the effort to refocus your attention will make changes in the brain and make it easier to focus on positive things in the future. As Norman Doidge (2008) writes,

> by paying constant, effortful attention and actively focusing on something besides the worry, such as a new, pleasurable activity, this approach makes plastic sense because it "grows" a new brain circuit that gives pleasure and triggers dopamine release which, as we have seen, rewards the new activity and consolidates and grows new neuronal connections. This new circuit can eventually compete with the older one.

New connections are made and old ones are weakened – focusing on negative things is replaced with focusing on positive things. You can "stay oriented in a positive, productive direction" (Gallagher, 2009). You can make the choice to direct your outlook to change your experience.

You can focus on one thing, or you can zoom out and see the bigger picture. You can make the choice. You can choose to focus on things that bring you joy and all that you are grateful for or you can choose to dwell on all that you lack,

> your ability to focus on this and suppress that is the key to controlling your experience and, ultimately, your well-being . . . and . . . to improving virtually every aspect of your experience, from mood to productivity to relationships.
>
> (Gallagher, 2009)

To do this we need to be in the habit of being constantly vigilant and ready to control the spotlight of our attention.

When you do take control of your attention you become more clear-headed and calm and feel more in control in general. You can take in what you want better, and respond in a more measured way. This increases confidence. You are then more able to create your life experience in the way you want within your circumstances.

Intentions

Attention can also be used to focus on the client's intentions in therapy, e.g. to get the most out of the session for their own benefit. Repeatedly focusing their attention on this can help to motivate them.

Redirecting attention to cope with difficult situations

Feeling more in control of your attention, you can use it to your advantage when you want a distraction to help you through difficult situations. For example, if you are about to be wheeled into an operating theatre for surgery, you can choose to be mindfully aware of all that is going on around you, or you can retreat to your own thoughts, distract yourself with happy memories or remembering trivial facts. In this situation, you can make a conscious decision to avoid focusing on the situation (when there is no benefit in facing it fully) and improve your ability to cope (e.g. avoid panic attacks).

Value attention

Consciously being aware of your attention gives you more power to choose your experience in the here and now; it is therefore something to be valued.

> The difference between "passing the time" and "time well spent" depends on making smart decisions about what to attend to in matters large and small, then doing so as if your life depended on it. As far as its quality is concerned, it does.
>
> (Gallagher, 2009)

When you reflect on this value with your client, it provides insight and motivation to pay attention to where it is at any given moment. It may not be possible to do this in all moments, but there is now incentive to increase awareness of it and take more control of it.

Developing attention

Attention is something that can and needs to be worked on to be able to use it consciously as much as possible. This can be done in several ways including:

- Adopting a good posture. This puts you physically in a state of readiness and alertness.

- Meditation, e.g. mindfulness of breath.

- Doing things you enjoy – practise fully engaging in something.

- Develop the habit of being mindfully aware of your attention – retrain your attention to be here, not there.

Attention is the key.

Summary

- What your attention focuses on creates your life in any given moment.

- Attention is the foundation skill for listening, learning and engaging in therapy.

- Increasing awareness of a client's attention – where it is in any moment versus where they want it to be – will help them to observe and understand their own attentional habits. This can help motivate clients to take more control over it to engage in therapy more effectively and improve their quality of life in general.

Activities

- Discuss attention with client. Engage with client, and reflect on their own attention to gain understanding of their attention and potential barriers/distractions. Ask the client if they have any concerns that are preoccupying them. Is there anything that could be resolved or talked through before you begin therapy? Or perhaps write the concerns down so the client doesn't need to worry about forgetting anything.

- Encourage the client to regularly consider where their attention is, and think about what they actually want to attend to. They could use post-it notes to remind themselves.

- Encourage the client to reflect on how it makes them feel when they are attending to something and consider if it is helpful and productive. Is there something more productive or positive to focus on that would be more beneficial for them and their sense of well-being?

- Encourage the client to develop attention using the above methods (see "Developing Attention" above).

- Practise moving attention to different stimuli – both inside and outside themselves, between thoughts, and different physical objects, then change from a narrow focus, e.g. on one object – to a scene, e.g. look out of a window. Encourage awareness of how their attention can be shifted, expanded and controlled consciously to alter their perspective on situations, e.g. from thoughts to emotions, to the body, to outside themselves and back to thoughts. Compare this with when attention is pulled by something such as a barking dog. Discuss how the client can do this to redirect attention from a negative and unhelpful focus.

- Anchor the self in the here and now. In *The Reality Slap* (2012), Russ Harris describes an exercise to redirect attention to the present moment for times when our attention gets swept along. This involves becoming aware of your feet on the floor, and standing or sitting up straight. Then slow the breath and become aware of things you can see and hear, and remember where you are and what you are doing.

References

Brantley, Jeff. 2011. Mindfulness FAQ. In Barry Boyce (ed.), *The Mindfulness Revolution.* Boston, MA: Shambhala Publications Inc., pp. 38–45.

Doidge, Norman. 2008. *The Brain That Changes Itself.* London: Penguin Books.

Gallagher, Winifred. 2009. *Rapt.* London: Penguin Books Ltd.

Harris, Russ. 2012. *The Reality Slap.* London: Robinson Publishing Ltd.

James, William. 1981. *The Principles of Psychology.* Cambridge, MA: Harvard University Press.

Malia, Kit and Brannagan, Anne. 2006. *Brain Tree Training Manual* received from the Cognitive Rehabilitation Workshop for Professionals.

18. Taking control, making choices

To take more control of our lives requires awareness.

Aims

- To understand how having a sense of little or no control over ourselves and our lives and not realising that we have, and are making choices adds to our feelings of stress and tension.

- To understand why we may not make conscious decisions.

- To explore what choices clients have/what choices they are making.

Understanding that there are always choices

Unaware of the choices we are making

We make many decisions throughout every day of our lives, but most of the time we are not aware of these. We don't take time to consider that things could have been done differently, which could have changed the course of events.

Everything we do involves choice and those choices affect outcomes.

There may be times though when we feel we have very little or no control over situations we are in and believe that we have no choices. We may feel as if we are on the conveyor belt of life, pulled along, resigned to our fate but not particularly happy (not fully accepting but not knowing what else we can do). Greg McKeown (2014) states,

we have overemphasised the external aspect of choices (our options) and underemphasised our internal ability to choose (our actions). This is more than semantics. Think about it this way. Options (things) can be taken away, while our core ability to choose (free will) cannot be.

We are always making choices, we are just not conscious of them,

in spite of all the things that happen to us that are outside our control, we are still, in large measure, "authoring" our own lives through our choices of response to such events and through what we initiate ourselves. In the process, we find our own ways to be in this world.

(Kabat-Zinn and Kabat-Zinn, 2011)

We are making choices, but we do not feel in control if we are not aware we are making them.

There is always a choice to be made every moment

We always have the ability to choose how to be and how to respond. As Viktor Frankl (2004) wrote, "everything can be taken from a man but one thing: the last of human freedoms – to choose one's attitude in any given set of circumstances, to choose one's own way." This choice cannot be underestimated as it affects your mood, others' behaviours towards you, how a situation plays out and your overall sense of well-being. You are more powerful in situations than you realise.

Being conscious of our choices

If we wake up to the choices we are making which keep us feeling like we are on the conveyor belt, we can begin to make conscious choices and take more control over our lives. "It is a matter of remaining conscious that we have a choice" (Jeffers, 2007). There may not be many options to immediately change our external circumstances but we can at least understand what we are doing and feel less powerless and frustrated. For example, even everyday issues, such as receiving an unwanted invitation, may make us feel that we have no choice but to go because we don't know how to politely decline with a straight up "no" or explain that we don't enjoy their company (how can we possibly say that?). But there is a choice being made – the one to avoid any upset or offence and the awkwardness of dealing with that. It is easier just to go. Or we may feel we do not have a choice about going to our dull job every day – but again a choice is being made, the one to keep a job which pays money and allows you to put a roof over your head and pay the bills.

Moment by moment our choices affect our lives.

When we drift along and are not fully conscious, we are unaware of there being such decisions. The key is to increase awareness and instead think about what we are really doing and the choices we are making.

Importance of taking control

Clients need to take ownership of the therapy process, to remember it is an opportunity for them. They can choose to make the most of it and get what they can out of it to try to achieve their goals. If they do not have awareness of the choices they are making, and of the fact that they are creating their lives in every moment through their thoughts, attitudes and choices, then they are a victim of their choices and the resulting consequences.

Taking responsibility

There is only so much that can be achieved if a client does not take full responsibility for themselves – their internal reality and their degree of participation in the therapy process. Our emotions and thoughts do not come from outside of us; we produce them inside ourselves. No one else can live our lives for us or think and feel for us. The power and the control ultimately lie within each of us, and this is where our locus of control needs to be.

Can the client possibly do more? What decisions are they making? Are they doing all they can to help themselves? Are they being a victim (giving their power away) or taking responsibility? What kind of moment are they creating for themselves? Taking control of ourselves and our lives takes effort – it means making our own decisions, changing habits/behaviours, and questioning, it "is the refusal to become a victim. It is the ability to focus on what you can control and not be distracted by what you cannot" (Brantley, 2003). Just making clients aware of this can initiate change in them. As Jill Bolte Taylor (2009) adds,

> You and you alone choose moment by moment who and how you want to be in the world. I encourage you to pay attention to what is going on in your brain. Own your power and show up for your life.

Focusing on values

As described in the chapter "Motivation", values are what are important to us in our lives, what we stand for, qualities we want to embody – they determine how we want to behave throughout our lives. For example, to be caring or courageous, loving or fun-loving, self-reliant or honest or any of the many other values listed by Russ Harris in his book *The Reality Slap* (2012). We may have many values, some of which may be more important than others to us.

Having values in our lives gives us meaning and purpose and drives us on through times and situations that we would otherwise recoil from and try to escape. "Saying yes [to whatever happens in your life] means getting up and acting on your belief that you can create meaning and purpose in whatever life hands you" (Jeffers, 2007). Values give us strength, energy, motivation and conviction to stand up and confront situations and do all we can, to do our best in the circumstances. They are the reason we put ourselves through things we would otherwise not. They are what allow us to develop ourselves and see what we can do when we push ourselves and try.

Values are an antidote to fear, ennui and a sense of powerlessness.

Values give us a positive focus which encourages us to give of ourselves, and therein lies our power as we are no longer concentrating on ourselves (our fears and perceived weaknesses), but something that is bigger than ourselves. In turn we develop inner strength and confidence as we push ourselves beyond our mental limits; "if we take the time to infuse our life with meaning, we are far less likely to give up on it when the going gets tough" (Harris, 2012).

Reasons to not take control and make conscious choices

Our ability to choose is simply forgotten

How can we forget our ability to choose? This again comes down to learned helplessness (see chapter: "Motivation"). Throughout our lives, at least in certain situations, we believe nothing we can do matters, and so we give up trying and go along with things (often unhappily). Our consciousness becomes weaker and a large part of our lives is spent on autopilot, with low expectations regarding our opportunities to make choices; therefore, we may not be on the lookout for them and ready to make them when we can. We have learnt to be so constrained, inhibited and well trained, in short "good" people, doing what's expected, mechanical, robotic, going through the motions, we have completely forgotten and are unaware of how much power we do have, the choices we can make and that the onus is on us to change – not others or life itself. As Greg McKeown writes in his book *Essentialism* (2014),

> When we forget our ability to choose, we learn to be helpless. Drip by drip we allow our power to be taken away until we end up becoming a function of other people's choices – or even a function of our own past choices. In turn, we surrender the power to choose.

Fear

> We fear what we can do as much as, if not more than, what we can't do.

This power we have can be frightening to exercise. To hold power is to have responsibility, because we have to be responsible for the consequences. We are afraid of what we can do and what will result from our choices and our actions – our potential. Our potential is an unknown, and the unknown can be daunting. Even though what we are doing and our circumstances may not be healthy or satisfying for us, it can be easier and feel more comfortable to stick with the familiar. But again, if you always do what you have done, you will always get what you've got.

Taking control and making choices

From Bruce H. Lipton, 2015, *The Biology of Belief* (10th Anniversary Edition).
Reprinted with permission.

To begin making more conscious choices, we need to "have a heightened awareness of our ability to choose" (McKeown, 2014). The less aware we are, the more likely we are to fall back on old patterns of thinking and behaviour rather than being open to other possibilities and making alternative (conscious) choices.

As taking control and making choices can be intimidating, there are ways to reframe our understanding of the process and our approach to it. In *Feel the Fear and Do It Anyway* (2007), Susan Jeffers describes the "No-Lose Model" which can move us from pain and fear to power and faith in ourselves. The emphasis is taken away from possible outcomes and redirected to what learning opportunities can be derived from choosing a particular option and its consequences. This way there is no right or wrong option, and so nothing to fear or regret, only plenty to experience and learn. Importantly, you learn you can handle more than you thought, which increases confidence.

Once we are aware of our choices, remember our values and manage any fears we have by learning to see decision-making more positively, we can start to take action. Just beginning to do this can lead to feeling more in control and more positive about taking control and to making conscious choices more and more in our lives.

Choices clients can make consciously

Clients will be making various decisions. Their options on the level of their physical and external world may be limited, but still there are choices being made. Many or all of these may be internal – their reaction to their situation.

Examples of choices

Where able, clients can make choices to improve their sense of well-being, such as:

- Doing things they find enjoyable as much as possible.

- Finding things to laugh about wherever possible/laugh as much as possible.

- Redirecting their focus to things such as the breath or enjoyable activities when they catch themselves in a spiral of overanalysing or dwelling on their problems.

- Generally focusing on things that are positive and reflecting on what they are grateful for as opposed to watching the news throughout the day and flooding their consciousness with the world's troubles, or focusing on their stories/beliefs and all that is lacking from their life, how life is different from how it is supposed to be. They can consciously choose to fill their mind up with positive or negative things.

- Cultivating their mind-set. To be open to learning, to be curious, to be able to change perspective/think flexibly.

- Responding mindfully – there are many different ways to react and respond. How do they want to react/respond? Observe, be aware and choose. Be open to considering other ways.

- Practising self-love and self-compassion.

- Practising affirmations, working on posture, practising breathing exercises/ mindfulness of breath, prioritising sleep, meditating/visualising regularly.

- Practising mindfulness – moment by moment being aware of their body and breath, thoughts and feelings, and the environment they are in. Using the body to help stay present – adopting a good posture, focusing the eyes, attending – this can help in making a strong connection with their internal and external realities in the here and now.

- Choosing to let go of old thoughts that do not serve to help them or make them feel good through mindfully watching and detaching from them and accepting them.

- Taking care of themselves – e.g. eating and drinking healthily, avoiding smoking.

- Choosing the people they associate with carefully where possible – who is supportive and positive, who is draining them?

- Focusing on working on themselves before trying to change others (when we change, those around us change also).

- Choosing active rather than passive activities, e.g. doing something creative or meditating versus watching TV.

- Learning about themselves and their minds and the power of the mind – to increase their feelings of control/power over self and lives.

In therapy

- Fully engaging in therapy sessions and the therapy process.

- Doing any given exercises between sessions.

- Raising their awareness of their own effort through self-evaluation (using self-rating scales to monitor effort level) and make a conscious choice to put more effort in if possible.

Choices being made about their circumstances

- Making physical changes, e.g. leave the situation or deal with issues with the relevant people.

- Separating internal reality from external reality – focusing on maintaining/regaining internal well-being no matter what is going on.

- Choosing their attitude – how do they approach life moment to moment? "We can't control the world but we can control our reactions to it" (Jeffers, 2007).

- Resisting or accepting.

- Noticing what and how they are communicating with the people around them – are they adding to the drama with their words and/or body language/facial expressions? What are they creating in their life?

- Choosing to observe and be fully aware of and engaged in the situation and involved in their care instead of tuning out. Are they on autopilot, or have they buried their head in the sand? Are they asking questions and making informed decisions?

- Choosing to dwell or make an effort to think more constructively and open their minds to alternative ways of dealing with their situation.

- Choosing to be proactive – are they doing all they can?

- Learning how to express themselves and their feelings.

- Choosing to take life by "the scruff of the neck" if able. Reenergise, regroup and take more control.

Clients have more power and control than they often realise, but they need to "Pay attention to each decision and detail in [their] life. Be present for each moment" (Beattie, 2003). They can choose to wake up to the life they have and the choices they have, and they can choose to make conscious choices and not be swept along in the usual way. Clients can observe and change their habitual ways of thinking and doing, and expand their awareness to see things in a different way. They can consider if there is anything that they can do, even if small, as this can be powerful and significant.

"Happiness depends upon ourselves."

– attributed to Aristotle

Summary

- We always have an ability to choose, even when our options are limited and none of them are desirable.

- There are always choices, but we are often not conscious that we are making them; they do not appear to be choices – we have learned to forget our ability to consciously shape our lives through the many choices we make every day.

- Increasing awareness of the choices we are making is the key to taking more control over our lives.

- Remembering our values and viewing decisions as opportunities to grow and develop instead of focusing on outcomes can help to reduce fear in taking control and making a decision.

Activity

- Encourage clients to think of what areas of their lives they have control over – even in small ways. Discuss how they have control over their thinking and their attitude. Remind clients about their values and how these can impact on how they feel and how they act. Make clients aware that they are making choices even when they feel they have none. Brainstorm together what choices they are consciously or unconsciously making. Do they want to change any of those choices? What choices are they making in the therapy process? (See examples of choices above.)

References

Beattie, Melody. 2003. *Choices*. New York, NY: HarperCollins.

Brantley, Jeffrey. 2003. *Calming Your Anxious Mind*. Oakland, CA: New Harbinger Publications.

Frankl, Viktor. 2004. *Man's Search for Meaning*. London: Rider & Co.

Harris, Russ. 2012. *The Reality Slap*. London: Robinson Publishing Ltd.

Jeffers, Susan. 2007. *Feel the Fear and Do It Anyway*. London: Vermilion.

Lipton, Bruce H. PhD. 2015. *The Biology of Belief 10th Anniversary Edition*. London: Hay House Inc.

McKeown, Greg. 2014. *Essentialism*. London: Virgin Books.

Myla and Kabat-Zinn, Jon. 2011. Parenting With Mindful Awareness. In Barry Boyce (ed.), *The Mindfulness Revolution*. Boston, MA: Shambhala Publications Inc., pp. 227–235.

Taylor, Jill Bolte. 2009. *My Stroke of Insight*. London: Hodder & Stoughton.

19. Acceptance, appreciation and moving on

Allow things to be as they are, from this point you can move on.

Aims

- To understand the significance and power of acceptance.

- To understand that arriving at acceptance is something that clients will do in their own time, as they are ready.

Unprepared for all aspects of life

We are prepared for a life of functioning on a day to day basis when things are running smoothly, doing our usual routines, with the usual people in our lives – family members, friends, colleagues and acquaintances – expecting tomorrow to be very much like today (our well-being comes to rely on our "normality"), and we are programmed to focus on doing and striving to achieve success and acquire things. We are led to believe life should be a certain way, and we are unprepared for when life veers from this expected course.

However, nothing and no one really belongs to us, nothing and no one is perfect and nothing and no one lasts forever. But we can often ignore these facts (even if subconsciously), we cling to our illusions and do all we can to hold on to our loved ones, our possessions, our health and our looks, i.e. the status quo. To live in this way is to live in denial – we are not prepared for the other side of our "happy ever afters", which is just as much a part of life. Suffering is inevitable when we attach ourselves to impermanent things. We are used to being shielded from the more challenging parts of life – we become comfortable and complacent, and just expect everything to be the same tomorrow as it is today.

Society doesn't usually like to focus on life's difficulties and that some of them will happen to us. We are not taught to understand the nature of life and prepare ourselves for life's inevitabilities. Loss and uncertainty happen; they are to be expected. Our expectations only add to our situations and suffering. In Russ Harris's book *The Reality Slap* (2012), he calls the difference between our beliefs and reality "the reality gap". The bigger the gap, the more suffering there will be. If we don't wake up to the realities of life, we are living in delusion, which only leads to pain.

Resistance

> **To surrender means to let go of the control you think you have in your life. It means releasing your preconceived ideas and notions about how you think your life should be. It is all about no longer forcing your personal will onto reality.**
>
> *Annemarie Postma*

From Annemarie Postma, 2013, *The Power of Acceptance*. Reprinted with permission.

If we do not like a situation, particularly if it is new and unfamiliar territory for us, we tend to respond with resistance in the form of an internal struggle that causes us further stress, tension, pain and anguish. This internal struggle can dominate our thinking and therefore our lives. It leaves little or no room for any other possible thoughts or feelings about the situation or anything outside of it. We believe that it shouldn't be, that we shouldn't have to suffer, which leads to a futile fight. We only create tension from trying to do battle with something impossible to battle with – the here and now, as it is. As Byron Katie (2002) writes, "The reason I made friends with . . . reality – is that I discovered I didn't have a choice. I realized that it's quite insane to oppose it . . . it hurts when I argue with reality [and] . . . I lose."

Reality is the truth, therefore arguing with it only causes stress and doesn't change the situation – it is not constructive. But when we believe that our thoughts and beliefs are important and true, it is hard to let them go and make room for reality, and that is when we clash with it. We then may not only cling to our thoughts about how our life should be, but also the thoughts about how bad it now is, which compounds suffering and distances us further from reality and deeper into thought. Our "shoulds" and "should nots" create problems for us without us realising.

> *We want to shape the reality of this moment, or the experience before us, into how we think it should be. We bring this struggle upon ourselves constantly.*
>
> Annemarie Postma

From Annemarie Postma, 2013, *The Power of Acceptance*. Reprinted with permission.

Acceptance

> *Use your energy to change your attitude towards the experience instead of trying to change the experience itself.*
>
> *Annemarie Postma*

From Annemarie Postma, 2013, *The Power of Acceptance*. Reprinted with permission.

Acceptance can be a difficult concept to understand. Resisting reality is comparable to non-forgiveness. Just like forgiveness, acceptance is a process that happens inside us, not in our external reality. It is not then about the external situation but about freeing ourselves from thoughts that resist what is happening in the now and the negative energy that is generated by these thoughts. As Louise L. Hay (2004) states, "The reality of true forgiveness lies in setting yourself free from the pain. It's simply an act of releasing yourself from the negative energy [that you are holding on to]." This is what we need to do to come to terms with our circumstances – consciously release the thoughts of how we think life should be.

> *Life is a series of natural and spontaneous changes. Don't resist them; that only creates sorrow.*
>
> *Let reality be reality. Let things flow naturally forward in whatever way they like.*
>
> *Lao Tzu*

Non-resistance

When you take away your beliefs about reality and allow things to be as they are, you are letting go of your resistance. We can make steps towards doing this by opening our minds to different ways of seeing and understanding reality, so that we begin to make space and allow for whatever is our present. By doing this you can begin to have a different relationship with reality – and it is no longer an enemy to battle with. "This doesn't mean that you condone it or approve of it. It just means that you can see things without resistance and without the confusion of your inner struggle" (Katie, 2002). It means making room for understanding and a better way of handling the situation.

> You are not pretending anything [e.g. all is fine]. You are allowing it to be as it is, that's all . . . we are not talking about happiness here . . . you cannot [always] be happy. It is impossible. But you can be at peace. There may be sadness and tears, but provided that you have relinquished resistance, underneath the sadness you will feel a deep serenity, a stillness.
>
> (Tolle, 2005)

The situation may not be your preference but you can go with it.

Facing reality

When we let go of our beliefs and turn our attention to what is, we can begin to see what really is there, rather than our distorted, and possibly catastrophised version of it. We are now living in reality rather than our thoughts and delusions. Reality is what it is and can be dealt with much more effectively when not blurred with imaginings and concepts which are not in alignment with it.

Our fixed ideas are familiar and give us a false sense of security and order about who we are and the life we are living. When we face reality we learn to let go of these notions and become more at ease with the unknown and the unfamiliar.

Facing the unknown of reality takes courage, but when you understand the nature of life you know pain and suffering are a part of life, that change is the only constant in life, and that there is a time for everything; you are more ready for these times and whatever they hold. Annemarie Postma (2013) adds,

> When you can say to yourself, "Pain and suffering are a part of life and I am not afraid to experience what is," then your whole relationship with pain and suffering will change. You may not see an immediate change in your direct surroundings, but you will begin to see life differently, and it will also feel different, because you are no longer ruled by suffering.

Adapting

Adaptation is "the process of becoming used to a situation" (Gallagher, 2009), whether "good" or "bad". Gradually, a new situation is seen differently. It becomes more normal as strong initial reactions pass. There is a more accepting and accommodating attitude and more space opens up to focus on other things.

> **" [It's not about letting] life waltz all over you, but rather an invitation to let go of our iron-fist control. "**
>
> *Annemarie Postma*

From Annemarie Postma, 2013, *The Power of Acceptance*. Reprinted with permission.

Acceptance is a process you have to go through. Time is needed to gradually release our hold on resistance and to relax into life as it is now. Kindness, gentleness and patience help through the process of "accepting your own humanness and frailty" (Ware, 2012).

Mindfulness and acceptance

Mindfulness "gives us a way to be with those situations when there is nothing more we can do to get away from the pain, when there is no alternative but to be with it" (Brantley, 2011). It is helpful in the process of acceptance because instead of trying to focus on the whole situation and worrying about every aspect of it (the now, the past and the future), attention is focused only in the here and now. Therefore any issues connected to the situation that is not in this moment are allowed to become dimmer as our minds become quieter and centred in the here and now, instead of magnifying the suffering.

Turning towards what *is* right now and embracing it, including what we are thinking and feeling, gives us an opportunity to learn "to relax into the reality of the current moment" (Postma, 2013). Jeff Brantley (2011) adds, "We can discover that the quality of mindfulness is not destroyed or damaged by contact with pain. It can know and relax with pain as completely and fully as it knows and relaxes with any other experience." This is surrendering to what is – full and total attention on a situation with full and total acceptance of everything you experience (including feelings of non-peace) and without judgement; this will give way to a sense of peace.

Paying attention to the now without judgement can be challenging initially, as you learn to go through pain instead of avoiding it (as you may, understandably, be in the habit of doing). But with practice it becomes easier to be with uncomfortable feelings and situations and to make space for them within yourself – so that they can be accommodated more easily with room to spare for other emotions and ideas.

Benefits of acceptance

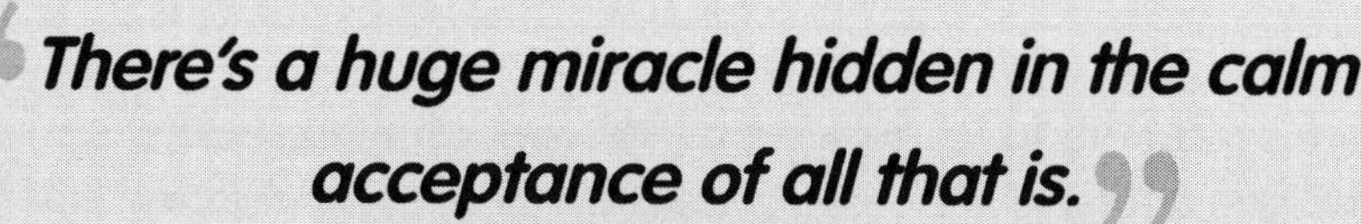

From Annemarie Postma, 2013, *The Power of Acceptance*. Reprinted with permission.

Acceptance and surrendering may feel like giving up, but really it is only a giving up of resistance, of the internal battle with what is, which causes unnecessary suffering. Acceptance is not passive non-action as in what results from learned helplessness – a giving up on attempting to do anything that can be done. Acceptance frees you up to see the situation with more clarity, calmly consider if there is anything to be done and act effectively. When you proceed from a point of acceptance your mind is free from the turmoil of resisting, you are then open to new fresh insights on the situation.

Surrender is a state of "peace and inner stillness" that you rest in when no action is possible, according to Eckhart Tolle (2006). Surrendering provides this peace through letting go of everything, so that external events no longer affect you in the same way. You are in a relaxed state, at ease. The benefits of this are not limited to simply feeling better but also helping you to stay healthier, heal better, have more energy and think more clearly – you feel more like yourself again. There is also space for more positive emotions to spontaneously arise. Thich Nhat Hanh (2008) describes surrender through this analogy,

> You are like a pebble which has let itself fall into the river, letting go of everything. . . . When you feel yourself resting like [the] pebble which has reached the riverbed, this is the point when you begin to find your own rest. You are no longer pushed or pulled by anything.

Trying to make sense of the difficult times and in the context of our lives

When we reach a stumbling block and life isn't what we wanted or expected, it can force us to look more deeply, to re-evaluate the way we have viewed life and have been living it. What we may come to realise is that life is a mystery.

> There is no explanation you can give that would explain away all the sufferings and evil and torture and destruction and hunger! You'll never explain it. You can try gamely

with your formulas, religious and otherwise, but you'll never explain it. Because life is a mystery, which means your thinking mind cannot make sense out of it.

(De Mello, 1990)

Life pulls us along in different directions. We can make choices in some matters but at other times we are swept along, simply led by life. We can find meaning and comfort in religion and spirituality, and we can create our own meanings. We can consider what life is asking of us in each moment rather than thinking about what life should be giving to us. We can view everything, everyone, every situation as a teacher, we can try to find out what we can learn from the experience. Good can come from bad. We can choose to take what we can from every situation.

Our task is to learn to be human, not perfect.

Appreciation

If life is always "OK" we run the risk of sleepwalking through our whole life. As De Mello (1990) writes, "Pleasant experiences make life delightful. Painful experiences lead to growth." Painful experiences can be our "wake-up call". They can be an opportunity for you to engage with life in a way that is different to normal (on autopilot going through the motions). You can choose to accept this challenge and be present for every moment and for every learning opportunity. We can question, we can look and we can search for answers. We can learn and grow and appreciate life in a different way.

> **New beginnings are often disguised as painful endings.**
>
> *Lao Tzu*

Gratitude

It is normal for us to take so much in our lives for granted. To consider most things as not very significant – just normal and mundane even. But on the other hand we may value things that are actually meaningless. Times of suffering bring life into sharper focus so that we can see what is really important – the people around us, the simple things like the breath, or just a sense of being alive. Life and every moment can now be precious. "A survivor appreciates life more" (Gallagher, 2009). Being grateful is a positive feeling and lends itself to a better sense of well-being.

Developing the inner self and inner strength

> **"*I thank whatever gods may be, for my unconquerable soul . . . I am the captain of my soul.*"**
>
> William Ernest Henley, 1891, *Invictus*

A poem Nelson Mandela used to recite to other prisoners while incarcerated at Robben Island prison.

Many people may consider what happens outside themselves the most important things to focus on; this reduces our power and control. If we start seeing these events as the transient content in life that they are, we can see that our internal reality is more important – our inner core which is constant and peace itself. Once you experience that, life is enjoyed in a new way. This perspective can also increase our sense of control, which adds to our feelings of well-being and our inner peace; we are able to let things go more readily.

> **"*[When we are] forced to [our] knees by life's difficulties, forcing [us], in turn, to travel the road inward and find a solution inward rather than finding one in the outside world.*"**
>
> Annemarie Postma

From Annemarie Postma, 2013, *The Power of Acceptance*. Reprinted with permission.

We may not have been introspective before, but if we have suffered enough and find that the old sense of security in the order of things no longer stands, it can force a change in attitude in order to find new ways of coping. We now have the opportunity to look inside and learn about ourselves. Life gives us opportunities to grow into the person we can be. To develop aspects of ourselves that have lain dormant – perhaps you can step up and do what is needed. To develop inner strength, grit even. We may come through feeling stronger and more confident in our ability to handle life's difficulties, as we are no longer dependent on external circumstances. Additionally we may also become more compassionate towards others, which we can use for the benefit of others, but this at the same time can be healing for ourselves.

Painful times also can prompt us to abandon our old thoughts and beliefs, our old sense of self – which cause much of our suffering, to know we do not need them and that they are not the source of our happiness. In fact we may realise we can't afford to have them as there is no room for dignity. So we let go of them, and we can now enjoy life for what it is without resistance, unease and in a state of wanting. With no mask to hide behind, no façade to keep up, this can be the moment of liberation.

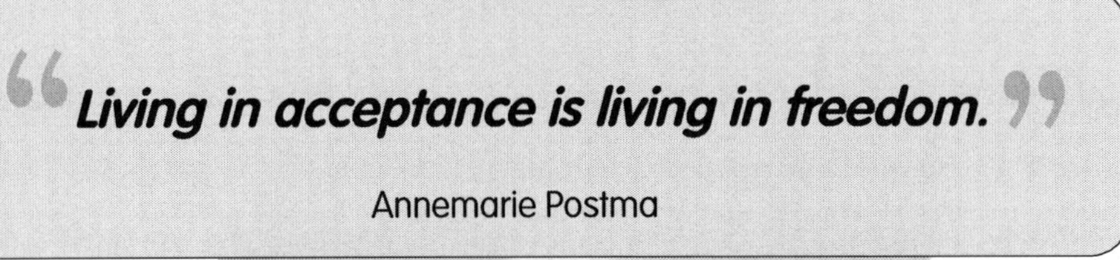

From Annemarie Postma, 2013, *The Power of Acceptance*. Reprinted with permission.

Moving on

Moving on mindfully simply means learning to live in the now, no longer encumbered by the baggage of your judgements, regrets about the past or concerns about the future. You may now have different views on life, and focus on doing different things. But fundamentally you are open to and present in the here and now.

A personal journey

Life is a journey; this is the clients'.

Arriving at acceptance is very much a personal journey. It comes from allowing time for the process to take place and personal insights gained on the way. It is not something that can be forced. Many of your clients may not be ready to accept and move on, and would not appreciate or benefit from any encouragement to do so. It therefore may be more appropriate to let clients talk about any resistance in their own time.

There are other books available which explore the concept of acceptance further. This chapter is primarily for background information to bear in mind, but it may also help facilitate conversations on the subject if they do arise. You may just need to sit and listen mindfully while clients express their resistance to what is. You can give them this space to be heard and help process their feelings, and you can inform clients that there are books available to help themselves with this journey. You can also be flexible with how you approach therapy; for example, you may work on things in a different order if they are not ready to deal with certain aspects of the presenting issue. These are ways you can work around non-acceptance, but if in doubt consider referring clients to an available specialist.

Summary

- Resistance to what is causes an internal struggle which can absorb a client's attention and creates stress and tension, making it difficult to focus on therapy.

- Acceptance leads to a sense of peace; it makes room for what is and an increased readiness for therapy.

- Acceptance is a personal journey which can take time, it cannot be forced.

References

Beattie, Melody. 2003. *Choices*. New York, NY: HarperCollins.

Brantley, Jeff. 2011. Mindfulness FAQ. In Barry Boyce (ed.), *The Mindfulness Revolution*. Boston, MA: Shambhala Publications Inc., pp. 38–45.

De Mello, Anthony. 1990. *Awareness*. Grand Rapids, MI: Fount Paperbacks.

Gallagher, Winifred. 2009. *Rapt*. London: Penguin Books Ltd.

Harris, Russ. 2012. *The Reality Slap*. London: Robinson Publishing Ltd.

Hay, Louise L. 2004. *I Can Do It*. Carlsbad, CA: Hay House Inc.

Henley, William Ernest. 1891. Invictus, published in *A Book of Verses*. New York, NY: Scribner.

Katie, Byron. 2002. *Loving What Is*. London: Rider Books.

Nhat Hanh, Thich. 2008. *The Miracle of Mindfulness*. London: Rider Books.

Postma, Annemarie. 2013. *The Power of Acceptance*. London: Watkins Publishing Ltd.

Tolle, Eckhart. 2005. *The Power of Now*. London: Hodder and Stoughton.

Tolle, Eckhart. 2006. *A New Earth*. London: Penguin Books.

Ware, Bronnie. 2012. *The Top Five Regrets of the Dying*. Carlsbad, CA: Hay House Inc.

20. Self-observation and self-awareness

Bedside manner

In each moment, observe how you can affect how your client responds.

Aims of chapter

- To understand the benefits of developing mindfulness when seeing clients.

- To understand the effects you are having on a client (your manner, words, body language), and how working on understanding yourself can lead to a greater sense of well-being for the client and lead to more productive therapy sessions.

Develop your own mindfulness practice

As you learn and consider the benefits of mindfulness practice for your clients, simultaneously begin to be aware of how it can also benefit you and those around you in your professional and personal life.

Just as your clients will be viewing the world through their tinted glasses, so will you unless you are aware of it. If you observe yourself carefully, you will detect assumptions, judgments and reactions about the people you come into contact with. You may on some level be vaguely aware of some of them, you may not like them and judge yourself for them, or try to repress them or justify them. These reactions occur because of the way you have been programmed through the course of your life to see the world.

As you develop your own mindfulness practice you will become aware of how your glasses are tinted; take them off, and see your client as they really are in that moment, not a filtered reality.

How do you begin doing this? Be mindful. Observe yourself in the third person; observe what is happening in you (reactions, emotions, tensions etc.) and in your external reality as though it were happening to someone else. Your inner thoughts and feelings and your outward behaviour are not personalised. Detach and allow yourself to see clearly – yourself and the situation you are in. As De Mello (1990, emphasis in original) writes,

> Wisdom occurs when you drop barriers you have erected through your concepts and conditioning. Wisdom is not something acquired; wisdom is not experience; wisdom is not applying yesterday's illusions to today's problems. As somebody said to me while I was studying for my degree in psychology . . . "Frequently, in the life of a priest, fifty years' experience is one year's experience repeated fifty times." You get the same solutions to fall back on: This is the way to deal with the alcoholic [etc.] . . . Wisdom is to be sensitive to *this* situation, to *this* person, uninfluenced by any carryover from the experience of the past.

Be constantly alert to the ever-changing reality you are in and understand your place in it, notice the effect you have on it and the people around you – how you are perceived. But the key is to observe in a detached manner, rather than a self-conscious, self-absorbed way, and as Gill Edwards (2010) points out, "acknowledge [your] own issues, and . . . sit easily and happily with the messiness of being human."

Understand yourself; if a client provokes a reaction – annoyance, anger, disgust – understand it – where does it come from? Understand and let go of it naturally – without judging yourself.

Reaching out and connecting

When a client comes to see you, you are automatically in a position of power. The client has an issue, and they hope you can help them. They don't even know you, but they are forced to trust you. They may be hopeful but uncertain of how the session will proceed, and likely on some subconscious level fear that you will not like them or will judge them negatively and perhaps help them less. The dynamic typically results in the client feeling vulnerable and perhaps being guarded; there will be distance between you.

When it comes down to it, though, when you first meet a client you don't really know what they are thinking, you don't know their background, you don't understand how they have been programmed to interpret other people's behaviour and how they will respond to you at any given moment. You can only begin to learn this by taking the time to reach out and make a connection with them. But you can be open to and ready for these feelings of anxiety about their situation and their appointment with you. You can show a willingness to understand them as a person in that moment, to show that you are fully with them, that you care, that you are going to do the best you can for them; you are thereby reaching out to them across the divide.

How to reach out

The way to connect with a client is to be fully present with them, fully conscious and open to everything as it is going on. *Listen, listen, listen. Listen with a neutral ear* (be neutral, there is no need to fuel any drama or suffering with pity). Carl Rogers emphasises the importance of listening in his book *A Way of Being* (1980), "when you are in psychological distress and someone really hears you without passing judgement on you . . . without trying to mold you, it feels damn good! At these times it has relaxed the tension in me." Carl Honoré (2005) adds, to this,

> the medical world is coming round to the holistic idea that people's mental state can affect their physical well-being. And once you accept that a patient is a person with moods, hang ups and a story to tell, it is no longer enough to run through a checklist of symptoms and reach for the prescription pad. You have to take the time to listen. You have to make a connection.

Practise active listening, so that you paraphrase back what the client says to make sure you have understood them correctly. Hear your client without judging (be aware of any judgements that do arise). What are they really saying? Take what they are saying seriously – what are their main concerns? Your client wants to feel heard. You need to be constantly vigilant, on your toes, alert, and in a state of openness, of not knowing, ready to learn and make decisions based on all the information you can gather. Build up as complete a picture as you are able about the person and the issue they have come to you with, and combine this with the knowledge you have acquired from your training and experiences so that you can see the client clearly and separate the client from their "story".

> A client needs to believe you are fully with them and that they are being heard.

Through your demeanour – your warm energy and your evident willingness to connect with the client as a person – you are able to draw the client out, because clients will know if you really want to do your best for them and are on their side. This will go a long way to helping reduce the client's stress, so that they feel comfortable to engage more openly and to offer up information that could be important in your management of their case. If they feel at ease and trust your intentions and knowledge, they will also more likely comply with advice and carry out therapeutic exercises independently.

Meet as equals

When you are fully present with a client, you are authentic and speak from the heart. We have all encountered health professionals as patients ourselves and been aware of feeling uncomfortable with them, feeling that you are a case to get through and move along as quickly as possible. They have not seen you as a fellow human being with feelings and concerns, but as just another case – a case of "here we go again." A role is being played, and as Tolle (2006) states, "Authentic human interactions become impossible when you lose yourself in a role."

When we take the time to consider clients, and people in general, we can see that we are all the same in terms of who we are rather than what we do. Take the time to recognise our "sameness". Recognise that all living beings have joys and cares just like you. We all have our issues and quirks. As Anthony De Mello (1990) writes, "Never mind 'I'm OK, you're OK' – 'I'm an ass, you're an ass!'" Humour brings you down to earth, and reminding ourselves of being the same in this way helps you to connect with clients on an authentic level; it helps keep your feet on the ground.

We also tend to focus on people who are close to us – family and friends – "my" son, "my" sister. But take away the "my". Try removing the concept of possession. Because in fact "my" son is not "mine" – he belongs to life. No one belongs to anyone; it is an illusion we cling to, that only death shatters. The people who are close to you in life you try to support because you happen to know them, and so your interest lies particularly with them, and you are more able to help them because of your understanding of them. But try to see everyone as a person; whether your mother or a stranger – because a stranger *is* a person you just don't happen to be familiar with. It is even possible that they *may* be a distant cousin you were unaware of. Consider that – they could be a family member and you don't know it. Either way, you can also imagine that the stranger is your niece/grandfather etc. then how would *you* want them to be treated by strangers in the same situation?

Be aware of any sense of power, of enjoying being the knowing one, the helper – be aware of the roles you are adopting – these are barriers to successful, and genuine, interactions. If you meet the client with humility and a genuine desire to support them, you will be rewarded with a more fulfilling session for both of you. It does nobody any good feeling above or removed from clients – because we are the ones "helping". In fact they are helping you too – to become the person you can be, and to experience the joy and satisfaction of helping. What you do to others, you do to yourself (karma – not in the sense of some mystical force but common sense, you bask in the energy you give out). When embodying kindness and warmth you are also benefitting from this positive energy – it feels good!

Partnership

A two-way street.

The tone of the relationship you develop with a client is very important – it will influence how a client responds to the therapy. Make it plain that you are there to work in partnership with them – as two adults, not an authoritarian type figure from childhood. Explore their case together. Encourage the client to think and judge whenever possible for themselves. Treating clients in this way will empower them and help them to retain their sense of dignity.

Be real, be authentic, be human.

Remember you are two equal human beings – talk like one. Beware of sounding like a textbook, as Alfie Kohn states in his book *Unconditional Parenting* (2005), "There's nothing worse than the hollow recital of a line learned in a book."

Be a companion – walk with your client on their journey – even if it is only briefly.

Empathy

You never truly know someone until you have walked a mile in their shoes.

Also be aware of other key aspects of your interaction with a client which shapes the relationship you have with them, including physical touch, your voice, eye contact, an ability to sit in silence when appropriate, and open body language. These are demonstrations of your humanity, your recognition of you both ultimately being the same – human – and which show your understanding of their feelings. They will be able to see that you have also known these emotions, because they are universal, and this connects you to the client; your client will sense that.

If you are becoming aware that you could be more compassionate with clients, be assured that it is something you can develop. When you work on empathy you are opening yourself to the client's suffering, you are increasing your awareness of it. By placing your attention on it and contemplating it you will understand your client better. Your behaviour towards them will alter naturally through awareness, because you will have a stronger desire to do what you can to alleviate their suffering, and you will be more motivated to maintain your attention on them throughout your interactions with them and for them.

Debriefing and tending to your own needs

Working with other people's suffering is different than dealing with your own, because it is not "mine", therefore there is some detachment. This detachment depletes less of your inner resources, and as the Dalai Lama writes in *The Art of Happiness* (1999), there is

a very high level of alertness and determination because you are voluntarily and deliberately accepting another's suffering for a higher purpose . . . a feeling of freshness rather than dullness. So the mental attitude makes a tremendous difference.

However, when you take on and share the suffering of clients you will need to make sure you are looking after yourself, so that over time you don't become overwhelmed with the clients' stories and draining energy. It is important to debrief with colleagues, to process your emotions, just as you may have allowed clients to do. If you don't acknowledge them and deal with them, they may affect you later, particularly if they are strong and you make a habit of harbouring your difficult feelings.

If the client or perhaps a colleague is causing you suffering through what they say or do, it is very important to remain fully present throughout any interactions in order to deal effectively with such people that you find difficult. You can take control; otherwise, the absence of your attention (consciousness) creates a void for the other person to fill – making the situation more difficult for you.

Being mindful of how you are feeling in your body and the emotions you experience can help you to identify anything negative that arises within you (from dealing with difficult situations and people) and be with it, understand it and allow it to transmute. Your emotions need to be heard. If they are not, they shout louder and communicate that your attention is needed by demanding it through physical ailments.

A counsellor once told me that they had supervision after every few sessions in order to debrief and this was considered vital for their well-being and to do the job effectively. Many therapists do not have access to that level of support but still take on the emotional baggage of their clients. You are not weak for struggling to deal with that if you are not supported. Seek out the support you need if you can. Use the techniques in this book to help yourself as well as your clients. Look after yourself and develop your own inner strength.

Summary

- How we interact with clients can significantly influence a client's response to therapy and their subsequent outcomes.

- We can inadvertently trigger reactions in clients which cause more stress.

- We need to closely observe ourselves with clients and the reactions we elicit to be more conscious of how we affect clients and to develop our ability to make them feel more at ease.

- As therapists, we also need to tend to our own needs.

Activities

- Do some mindful breathing for a few moments before seeing a client.

- Affirm your intention before each session, e.g. "I am ready to listen fully" or "I intend to help as much as I can."

- Contemplate the client's feelings and suffering (known and surmised) to develop and maintain your compassion.

- If you have been in the profession a long time, demoralised from it all – same old clients, office politics etc., take time to remember why you went into the profession in the first place.

- Reflect on your observations of yourself with a colleague during peer supervision.

- Reflect on our common humanity, our "sameness". As you walk about outside or perhaps when shopping, take the time to really notice people. Reflect on the fact that each person you come into contact with will have their own hopes, joys and worries. See the human. Reflect on these significant similarities and consider how superficial differences are trivial in comparison.

References

De Mello, Anthony. 1990. *Awareness*. Grand Rapids, MI: Fount Paperbacks.

Edwards, Gill. 2010. *Conscious Medicine*. London: Little, Brown Book Group.

HH Dalai Lama and Cutler, Howard C. 1999. *The Art of Happiness*. New York: Penguin.

Honoré, Carl. 2005. *In Praise of Slowness*. New York, NY: HarperOne.

Kabat-Zinn, Jon. 2013. *Full Catastrophe Living*. London: Bantam Books.

Kohn, Alfie. 2005. *Unconditional Parenting*. New York, NY: Atria Books.

Rogers, Carl. 1980. *A Way of Being*. New York, NY: Houghton Mifflin Company.

Tolle, Eckhart. 2006. *A New Earth*. London: Penguin Books.

Conclusion

Your client seeks help from you for their "problem", as they see it, but their response to the problem and hence their readiness for therapy is affected by their thoughts and beliefs which have been brought about by their conditioning. Consequently, you can assume that most of your clients will be experiencing stress to some degree and would benefit from addressing it, as long as they are ready to do so.

Stress and tension reflect an ongoing difficulty in dealing with our life's circumstances. This book is relatively broad in scope to increase understanding and awareness of why these difficulties are so prevalent, and to put them into context. It is fundamentally about learning how to cope in our society, to help release some pressure that has built up due to a lack of awareness. We unconsciously rely on older generations to model for us, and we follow their lead. But as this society we live in has evolved so quickly in relatively recent history, it is more pertinent to take the time to consider how to approach life and to have an awareness of what we can expect from life, and how to not only survive, but thrive when possible.

This book discusses the larger context, including how unconsciousness has its roots in childhood. It aims to encourage clinicians to recognise how we are all affected, how typically unconscious we all are. See yourself in your client. We are separated by a matter of degrees. With this understanding, the idea is for therapists to develop a personal interest and go on to read more on the subject, potentially starting a journey of self-discovery. If you think this is for you, then you will be motivated to learn more, eventually internalising the information and developing your own awareness. Your approach and manner towards your clients will be coloured as a result and you will be more authentic with them. But be aware that it is easy to read this book once and perhaps think "Yes, interesting" and then forget about it. Mindfulness and awareness need to be made a part of your life in order benefit from them. It is about being conscious all the time, staying alert and being ready for all possibilities in a situation. It needs commitment.

The information provided here is not meant for in-depth discussions on philosophy and existentialism with clients but to help prompt and facilitate dialogues, to point out obvious truths which will strike a chord with them. This will allow for a shift in perspective and attitude and create a different understanding of themselves, their reality, and their relationships with themselves and their circumstances. You may only use a fraction of what you have read with any given client due to timing (the client is not ready), time restraints, inappropriateness [due to the nature of your relationship with them/your role] or the client is unwilling and not open to discussing anything of "depth." It is important to proceed gently with clients – don't force any subjects or relaxation practices. It is for you to internalise and introduce and use as appropriate. Even if it is only your own understanding and awareness that develops, this will increase your empathy for your client, hence your effectiveness as a clinician. It is ultimately down to you to discern which clients would benefit from the issues discussed in this book, which aspects would be effective, to what depth you go with them and when to introduce them. This is down to your professional judgement combined with your own mindful awareness.